Controversies in Sociology
edited by
Professor T. B. Bottomore and Professor M. J. Mulkay

11
A
Third World
Proletariat?

Controversies in Sociology

A
Third World
Proletariat?

PETER LLOYD

London
GEORGE ALLEN & UNWIN
Boston   Sydney

**George Allen & Unwin (Publishers) Ltd,
40 Museum Street, London WC1A 1LU, UK**

George Allen & Unwin (Publishers) Ltd,
Park Lane, Hemel Hempstead, Herts HP2 4TE, UK

Allen & Unwin Inc.,
9 Winchester Terrace, Winchester, Mass 01890, USA

George Allen & Unwin Australia Pty Ltd,
8 Napier Street, North Sydney, NSW 2060, Australia

First published in 1982

British Library Cataloguing in Publication Data

Lloyd, Peter
    A Third world proletariat? – (Controversies in sociology; 11)
1. Underdeveloped areas – Poor
2. Underdeveloped areas—Cities and towns
I. Title   II. Series
305.5'6   HC92

ISBN 0-04-301140-3
ISBN 0-04-301141-1 Pbk

Set in 11 on 12 point Times by Red Lion Setters, London
and printed in Great Britain
by Billing and Sons Ltd, Guildford, London and Worcester

Contents

Preface

The 'Third World' has become a convenient euphemism for the poor nations of the world, widely differing though they are in their cultural background and their degree of poverty. Indeed, some would today distinguish a Fourth World whose stagnation contrasts with the slow development of the Third. My focus in this book is upon countries most of which lie in the tropics, have an indigenous or non-Western cultural heritage and have experienced colonial rule. My emphases reflect the available literature – much more has been written about social class in Latin America and Africa (though from differing perspectives) than in Asia or the Middle East.

My topic, though apparently a succinct one, is vast – for class embraces such a multitude of aspects of social life. My task is to pose questions rather than to provide answers. In no sense is this book a survey of all available literature, assessed and evaluated to provide a true and accurate picture of a real world. Were such a picture possible for one country, it would not be true even for its close neighbours let alone for those in other continents. Yet these countries are, in a most generalised manner, undergoing similar processes of change. Whilst recognising some universals in our analysis of class, we must be aware of a host of factors which contribute to diversity.

Such diversity promotes inconclusiveness; the urban poor in one country may be much more like a proletariat than those in another. Furthermore interpretations of the evidence are ideologically charged; in identifying a proletariat one may contribute towards its self-consciousness; one may equally raise false hopes of its political strength. The task of the scholar is to delineate the range of variables which must be evaluated in each situation.

Inevitably this book reflects my own background and

experience. An interest in social class, latent since my student days, was reawakened in western Nigeria as I contrasted Western analyses with the urban Yoruba perceptions of their own society. It was fostered as I studied the growth of shanty towns in Lima, Peru. Throughout I have tried to blend the approaches of sociology and social anthropology.

1

Introduction

Is there, in the cities of the Third World, a proletariat? With the rapid urban development of recent decades and the increasing wage employment in manufacturing industry and the public services, has a working class been created?

In posing these and like questions we are applying to the Third World concepts which developed in Europe in the nineteenth century – a class terminology used by scholars and laymen to categorise populations and illuminate the historical process. But are these concepts specific to time and place? Most would now answer – no. Some would argue that the processes of economic development now taking place in the Third World replicate those of the industrial nations of the West and that the social structures of the former are converging towards those patterns visible in the latter. Others would stress the universality of the concepts – inequality and exploitation exist everywhere; some Marxists now describe the elders and youths in a tribal society as opposed classes (for example, Terray, 1975; but see also Hindess and Hirst, 1975, ch. 1). Class analysis is thus appropriate not only in the pre-industrial stages of our own culture but in widely different cultures too.

In recent years Western scholars, mostly those of a Marxist persuasion, have increasingly used class terms in their analyses of Third World societies (for example, Horowitz, 1970; R. Cohen, 1972; Kitching, 1972; Gutkind and Waterman, 1977). Some of these have been armchair theorists, others have conducted intensive empirical studies in the field – the diversity of their findings in some measure reflects their methods. African and Asian scholars, writing of their own countries, have been slow to follow suit; most seem wedded to the theoretical frameworks dominant in the 1950s. Latin American scholars, however, in attempting to account for the continued backwardness of their continent, have developed modes of class analysis both within and outside the overarching concepts of dependency and marginality (for example, Germani, 1980; see also Cardoso and Faletto, 1969; Nun, 1969; Zenteno, 1973, 1977; O'Brien, 1975; Touraine, 1976).

In questioning the validity of class analysis in the Third World we are doing much more than engaging in intellectual casuistry. The concepts which we employ are rich in associations. A term such as proletariat conjures up a myriad of images (perhaps not identical for all of us), far beyond any limited definition. In categorising a person as a member of the proletariat we immediately assume certain modes of behaviour; a proletariat is assumed to play a specific role in history. But if we assign such terms on the basis of poor or inadequate evidence our predictions are likely to be frustrated. Class is, indeed, such a complex phenomenon that accurate prediction is, on the basis of this concept, impossible. Categorisation in class terms is, too, a political act designed to present and substantiate an interpretation of the world about us. If we accept an analysis of a situation in class terms we shall act in a specific manner towards given goals. To give a simple example: if the urban poor of a Third World metropolis see themselves as a proletariat, they will redouble their efforts in collective organisation; if they are seen as a proletariat by foreign or international working-class movements, money and other assistance will be offered to them to pursue the revolutionary struggle. Class analysis is praxis.

Our initial question is not as simple as it may appear—it subsumes three questions. First, what is happening in the Third World? How far *do* the characteristics of the urban poor replicate those observed elsewhere? Secondly, what do we mean by a social class? Rival analytical frameworks compete with each other, and there is usually less disagreement about the empirical details of social reality than about the broader concepts through which it is understood. Thirdly, our own analysis may not be shared by, and indeed may not be comprehensible to, the actors involved; the city migrant in the Third World has been socialised into a traditional rural culture in which the very concept of inequality may differ markedly from that which we accept. How far are we justified in speaking of a social class which has no consciousness of its own existence?

Let us look at each of these questions a little more closely. Industrial capitalism developed autonomously in the West; social and economic developments in the Third World have been dependent upon the West. Although the states of Latin America threw off the colonial yoke long before it fell upon those of Africa, recent developments in each continent have, in a most general sense, been remarkably uniform. Initially the Third World countries provided the raw materials for Western industry, either from foreign-owned mines or plantations, or from local peasants. Latterly foreign and multinational companies have felt it profitable to establish manufacturing industries in the Third World, both taking advantage of cheap labour to produce goods for export and serving a local market with the production or assembly of consumer goods. Capital and technology are imported; interest and dividends must be repaid; local research and development are absent. Contemporaneously the mass of the population have been drawn further into the political and social life of the state. Universal suffrage has been granted; health and education services have been widely extended. If we are to seek analogies with the West, should we be making the comparison with the early decades of the nineteenth century when, as in the Third World today, a relatively small proportion of the labour force was in industrial employment, or with the present day, when employment is to be found in large companies or public bureaucracies and when a very substantial proportion of the workforce is employed in the public service sector? The consequence of the penetration of the rural areas by these social and economic changes is well known — it results in a flood of migrants to the cities. Arriving with neither skills nor money, they find insufficient jobs awaiting them. A few find stable and relatively well-paid wage employment; many receive a meagre minimum wage – secure in the case of public employees, insecure in the case of building construction workers. Many have no alternative but to exploit niches in the so-called informal sector, becoming self-employed artisans, traders, or petty professionals and providing goods and services for both rich and poor. In describing this sector as marginal, many have assumed that it would wither away as increased investment provided more wage employment. Others have more recently argued that this sector is in fact dependent upon the formal sector (of highly capitalist industry and state bureaucracies) subsidising it through the provision of cheap goods and services; its continued existence is therefore assured. The scenario in the Third World state thus consists of a dominant and comparatively very rich stratum of political leaders, civil servants and, in many countries, military leaders who own neither industry nor the land; their control is severely constrained by the international economic system in which they have a negligible participation. The entrepreneurial stratum – a bourgeoisie – is small; few local businessmen have large companies, and while some of these compete with foreign firms others are their agents; others too are employed in a managerial capacity in the foreign firms. Much less affluent is the large stratum of white-collar workers, which consists of junior executives, teachers, and the like. The 'urban poor' generally comprise three-quarters of the city's population, embracing the relatively well-off employees and prosperous independent craftsmen and the very poor spasmodically employed labourer and itinerant petty trader. In the rural areas the peasantry is variously divided according to wealth, land holding and employment of labour. This peasantry outnumbers the urban poor.

We have here a pattern of stratification clearly different from that of Western nations in either the nineteenth or the twentieth century. The dangers inherent in applying Western concepts and then assuming congruence with Western forms will be obvious. Yet this does not mean that we cannot use the Western concepts to explore the characteristics of Third World stratification, perhaps modifying the concepts in the process. That is the task of this book. For reasons of space, the discussion must be limited to one specific stratum – the urban poor/proletariat/working class. Class theorists are agreed, however, that social classes can exist only in conjunction with one another – whether one sees classes as empirically observable categories of people showing common characteristics or, more abstractly, as a pattern of relationships between such categories. So here we must describe both the characteristics of our selected stratum and its relationship with the rest of the society.

People and events exist in the real world; social classes are mental constructs by which we attempt to create order, a patterned regularity, in what we observe. The validity of these constructs lies variously in their predictive capacity, their simplicity and elegance, or their conformity with our personal ideology – and in the case of class concepts it is perhaps the last which dominates. Such concepts, and the propositions by which we interrelate them, are continuously changing as we seek more satisfactory ways of interpreting the world. Most current academic debate on social class derives originally from the writings of Marx and Weber (see, for example, Parkin, 1971, 1974b; Giddens, 1973; Crompton and Gubbay, 1977; Benson, 1978) and, substantial as is the overlap between them, it has polarised into definitions of class in terms of man's economic role in production and definitions in terms of status, his patterns of consumption and life-style. The debate progresses with the continual elaboration and refinement of the basic terms: the discovery of unpublished or unknown manuscripts leads to reassessment of their authors' beliefs and intentions. This progression is set against the swing in the pendulum of dominant paradigms. The structuralism of Talcott Parsons gives way to a French variety in which Marxists such as Althusser and Poulantzas have reformulated class analyses. The determinism of the latter is countered by the actor-oriented phenomenological approach, derived through Schutz from a hitherto less strongly emphasised vein in Weber's writings, and facilitating a new approach to the concept of class-consciousness. The real world, too, is changing, as the dark satanic and owner-managed mills of the early nineteenth century give way to the technologically advanced and salubrious factories of the giant corporations. New categories of worker emerge: the affluent worker enjoying amenities previously associated with an 'upper-middle class'; the white-collar clerks who lack any career opportunities; at the top the managers and highly skilled technicians; and at the bottom the immigrant, more often defined in ethnic than in class terms (or else deemed to belong to an underclass, marginal to the accepted pattern of class structure). Thus in attempting to apply class terms in our analysis of Third World societies we are using concepts which are continually changing; indeed, our own efforts in this direction will probably contribute to the changes.

Scholar-analysts of class structure have conventionally held the arrogant, though perhaps justifiable, view that their concepts are more precisely defined, their sources of information more extensive, than those of the actor; the arrogance of those who dogmatically assert that their own theories are correct is still greater. The 'objectivity' of the observer is juxtaposed with the 'subjectivity' of the actor whose view of the world is seen to be based, so often, upon bias, misinformation, or false consciousness. As a result class-consciousness has been neglected as a field of study even by Marxists for whom it assumes so central a role in the revolutionary struggle; recent studies of working-class images or models have gone largely unnoticed in the Marxist literature. The antipathy towards the actor's view of the situation stems perhaps from an assumption that observer and actor hold equally valid views – resulting in cultural relativism. But such an assumption seems unwarranted. The observer must prefer his own view, although in modesty he recognises the existence both of other scholarly approaches and of those of the actors, accepting that he might learn from these. His analysis of a situation is enhanced, however, when he appreciates the manner in which the actor's own interpretation of his situation conditions his activity. The observer, however, is perhaps better placed both to see the constraints in the real world within which the actor operates and to anticipate the unintended consequences of his actions. To distinguish clearly between one's own view of the world and that of the subjects of one's study is a difficult task; it takes one form in the West where scholar and people are using the same class terminology, though perhaps with different definitions or degrees of precision, another in Third World situations where our class terminology is quite alien to the culture of the urban migrant.

The organisation of this book reflects the form in which the questions have been posed in the preceding pages. We cannot start looking for classes in the Third World until we know what we are looking for. This may seem an incredibly trite remark, but much of the debate so far seems to have been between protagonists who talk past each other, using different definitions and, perhaps, merely reaffirm an ideological position. In the next chapter I want, in a most simplistic manner, to establish what seem to me to be the major issues in current debates on class – getting behind the various Marxist and Weberian theses rather than elaborating or testing them. Thus the focus of class analysis may rest at different levels: either at an abstract structuralist level with emphasis on a pattern of relationships, or at a level of empirically observed social categories. Classes may be defined in economic/production or social/consumption terms; and in as much as the substantial congruence of these two forms of class is accepted, their relationship must be explained. How many classes does one find? And what is the relationship between them: dichotomous, hierarchical, or functional? The simplification of the structural pattern contrasts with the complexity of the real world – so classes are subdivided (as in Lloyd Warner's six-class schema) or viewed in historical progression, the incongruous elements seen, as by Marxists, as classes in decay or in formation. Actor's models have usually been held to be of a different order from those of the observer; I would analyse both in the same manner. Actor's models are indeed less precise in their formulation; but the point to be emphasised seems, to me, to be the multiplicity of models used by the actor in specific situations. As I have described elsewhere (Lloyd, 1974) he uses both ego-oriented and externalised models; he has, too, a view of the world as it is and as it might be. If one stresses the significance of actor's models, and if one accepts that the concepts, attitudes and so on, which constitute them derive not solely from the actor's current work situation but from his whole life experience, the study both of social mobility and of social relationships outside the work situation assumes a new importance. Class-consciousness strictly means consciousness of *class*, rather than of other groupings or relationships. The current debate obliges us, indeed, to broaden the question to seek the ways in which inequality is conceptualised. Attempts to formulate degrees of class-consciousness seem agreed in a division between awareness and action – the effort to further class (or, by implication, other) interests. All class activity is political; but political party membership notoriously fails to correspond closely with class groupings. Parties reflect a great variety of interests. Political movements have a life of their own, their development often failing to correspond closely with changes in class composition and relationships. Marxists have for a long time assumed the subordination of the political sphere to the economic; they now debate its relative autonomy (Hunt, 1977).

With such issues in mind we can both begin our own analysis of the Third World situation and appreciate the underlying assumptions of those who have already contributed to the debate. We look first at the economic and social changes currently taking place: the development of manufacturing industry, the increasing urbanisation and the many concomitants of these phenomena. An overview of attempts to explain this process, in terms, for instance, of dependency, shows that some theories ignore class formation while others stress the peculiarities of its development in the Third World. In looking at the organisation of production we shall see that wage-earners in industry and the public services fall readily into our Western categories. The small-scale artisans, traders and professionals who form such a large part of the urban poor are an anomaly. They usually own their tools; they exploit family members, apprentices, or journeymen; they have aspirations which we could term 'petit bourgeois'; their linkage with the large-scale capitalist or 'formal' sector takes varying forms; but since their production is relatively small, the surplus extracted from them is small too. Thus, it is argued, whilst wage-earners in the 'formal' sector are exploited, these people are prevented from producing; they are, in the terms of some Latin American writers, marginalised. How does one categorise such people in class terms?

Two features characterise the mobility of the Third World urban poor. One is the peasant origin of so many of them – they were initially socialised into traditional rural values, and they see their successful adaptation to urban life as an advancement (Mangin, 1970; Southall, 1973). Secondly, with the substantial size of both formal and informal sectors, movement of individuals between them is considerable – a typical migrant might work casually for an artisan before finding stable wage employment, but then aspire to set up on his own account. The migrant aspires to relatively prosperous self-employment for himself, and in schooling his children, hopes that they will enter the ranks of clerks and teachers. But whilst upward mobility for some is possible, the constraints in the situation seem likely to doom most aspirations to failure.

The ambiguous economic position of those in the informal sector has tended to highlight their other social relationships, but these are, of course, equally relevant for wage-earners. First, the family unit: one frequently finds a man engaged in two or more forms of activity in an attempt to raise his income; his wife and children may help him in his own work, but may equally be independently occupied, the variety of their income sources providing a safeguard against individual unemployment. Secondly, the close links between the migrant and both his family in his village of origin and his co-villagers in the city have been repeatedly stressed. One may explain the continuance of such relationships in affective terms, but one important function is to provide economic security. The strength of these ties may be manipulated by politicians who thus raise ethnic consciousness. Ethnicity and class have been seen as incompatible forms of social grouping, but we must distinguish between conceptual incompatibility and that deriving from the finite amount of time and money to spend on activities directed to class or ethnic ends. The third important social grouping is the residential unit; in the shanty town (although not in the inner city slum) active ward organisations have often been reported. Radicals, both in the West and in the Third World, have tended to denigrate such community activity as being inimical to class formation. Most crassly it is argued that in ameliorating local conditions the ultimate protest against abject poverty is postponed; communities see themselves as competing one against another rather than working towards common goals. It has, however, been pointed out in the West that community organisations involve many who are outside trade union organisations and have no other avenue of protest; autonomous community activity should therefore be fostered, both as a means of achieving immediate ends and as a mode of educating people about the reality of the social structure which creates the problems they are seeking to solve. Such a viewpoint is even more pertinent to the Third World city where, for an even larger proportion of people, the ward organisation is the prime arena of political activity, the one arena in which government impinges directly upon them. Yet it remains difficult to transform community competition into a united protest against the injustices experienced.

The accounts of political activity among the urban poor have varied in their focus. Scholars who have worked in the shanty towns emphasise the individualistic concern with personal achievement and the belief that success, not only of the self-employed, lies in the manipulation of patrons. The ills of society are laid at the door of a diffusely defined 'government' rather than at that of 'capitalism'. Leaders variously epitomise these attitudes and seek benefits through bargaining with, rather than opposing, government. The dominant groups in the society reinforce these attitudes through stressing either self-help or dependence on government. The attempts made by parties to mobilise the urban poor reflect the overall class configuration of the country; but the form which these attempts take constitutes an essential element in the creation of class-consciousness.

We may seem to be covering a vast part of the life of the poor. But classes, it is generally agreed, incorporate economic, social and political elements.

Debates about class formation in the Third World cluster around a small number of issues, all illuminated by points raised above. First, the scope of the working class: some would confine the term to wage-earners in industry, perhaps assuming that this is an emergent class which will eventually increase to a size comparable to that in Western industrial societies; others, anxious to establish a simple dichotomous class structure, define a working class which includes not only all the urban poor but also the peasantry – the modes of their exploitation being similar to those of the urban poor, however different their social and political activities.

Allied to this is a second issue: the divisions within the urban poor between those in stable, well-paid employment – a 'labour aristocracy', and the very poor and insecure – the 'lumpenproletariat' or 'marginals'. How does one categorise these divisions and what is the relationship between them?

Thirdly, the rural origins and links of the urban poor: variously their 'peasant mentality', their lack of urban commitment shown in their desire to return to the village, their strong links with co-villagers rather than workmates, make even the industrial wage-earners fall short of being

Fourthly, the interpretation of protest: workers go on strike but their demands, as understood by observers in the field, may be merely for limited wage increases; visions of a socialist society may be imputed to them by those distant from the events. In looting the city centre the urban poor probably lack a clear vision of their objectives.

But Third World governments are fragile, and strikes and mob violence may well lead directly to their collapse – a consequence perhaps unintended by the poor. The succeeding regime may be more conservative and repressive, or more radical; if the latter, some observers will be sure to claim the success of the class struggle. But, one must ask, how far must the struggle exist consciously in the minds of the people? How far can it be a reified 'force of history'?

Our opening question – is there a Third World proletariat? – cannot have a simple answer. The Third World is not homogeneous. Some countries have enjoyed a much greater degree of industrialisation than others – witness, for example, recent designations of a Third and Fourth World, the former being on the development road, the latter doomed to eternal poverty and stagnation. In some countries economic development is taking place within an already stratified society (ethnic divisions sometimes reinforcing other social distinctions); in others it is a tribal society which is being transformed. Latin America is here contrasted with tropical Africa.

Our main task, however, is to ask how far the changes ongoing within the Third World may be illuminated by the use of class concepts. Not 'are the urban poor a working class?' but 'in what respects are the urban poor like our conception of a working class?'. Is our class terminology a valuable tool for analysis? Or does it merely provide vague descriptive labels, replete with misleading connotations or slogans for political mobilisations (valueless if the recipients of the message do not understand it)? Our efforts may lead us to redefine our concepts so that they are analytically useful not only in the Third World but also in studies of our own society. For instance, our stereotype of the Victorian worker as poor but radical has recently been sanctified by Goldthorpe *et al.* (1969) in their typology as the 'traditional worker'. Several scholars have stated their inability to find such a being in existence today; Giddens (1973, pp. 199–200, 211–12) accepts that he did exist in the early periods of industrialism, though Westergaard and Resler (1975, pp. 392ff.) argue that at this period the worker was locally oriented and lacked the universalistic vision implied in the definition. If he exists at all the traditional worker should, by such reasoning, be found in the cities of the Third World. A failure to find him there may well show how different the findings of the historian using contemporary political pamphlets may be from those of the sociologist working among the people studied. Who is right?

2
The Class Debate

Social class is one of the many constructs by which we seek to make sense of the world around us, trying to find order and patterns of regularity in the infinite variety of our experiences. With it we categorise people and in the events which constitute their interaction we postulate the relationships that link them. But although the use of class terminology is widespread we do not all necessarily employ a common set of constructs. Classes are defined in diverse ways and in arguing for their existence or non-existence we often talk past each other; agreement can only rest upon shared meanings.

What, then, are these constructs which we employ? What are we arguing about? Our first task must be to define the issues under discussion. We might perhaps aspire to a culturally neutral position, seeking a set of terms and ideas with which to evaluate social class constructs wherever they appear. But we cannot avoid completely our own intellectual heritage. Most of the discussion of class in contemporary industrial society derives from Karl Marx and Max Weber; some engage in critical exegesis of their classic texts to determine what their authors really meant; others attempt to apply their apparent basic premises to the contemporary scene. The jargon of each school becomes elaborated as scholars seek to refine and elaborate each concept. The difficulty of their task is compounded by the uncertainties and ambiguities in the classic texts. Marx, as we are so often told, never set out a theory of class and the fundamental structural dichotomy employed, for instance, in his more apocalyptic writing contrasts with the more complex class schemata employed in his analysis of the political events of his time – events in which other oppositions were manifest.

In this chapter I shall try to outline some of the basic principles and issues which underlie the present debates about social class. I shall do so in a most simplistic and cavalier manner, for in such a short space it is impossible to do justice to the ideas which I have used; nor can their philosophic implications be explored. But in as much as the task of this book is to evaluate the usefulness of applying our Western class concepts to the urban poor of the Third World, we must specify the nature of these concepts.

On many issues there is a substantial measure of agreement. Social class is important and significant; witness the number of books and articles written about it, the ubiquity of class terminology in our everyday discourse. It concerns the social inequality in our societies and the unequal distribution of rewards to members of a given society, whether these rewards be in the form of material goods, leisure facilities, honours, or prestige. Such distribution yields a social ranking of individuals. Power may be implicit or explicit. Some would see power as a form of reward; for others power resides in those people who can maintain the rules of distribution, the patterns of ranking. It becomes the major determinant of inequality.

Social class cuts across the arbitrarily defined fields of political, economic and social activity. It embraces too all members of a society; it is not possible to have a minority which is 'unclassed'. It exists from generation to generation although not in an unchanging form; individuals may, however, move into and out of specific classes with varying ease.

Social class, however, refers not merely to what people are, but also to what they do; it denotes patterns of action. As Poulantzas (1973b) has said, 'classes exist only in the class struggle', thus advancing Marx's own dictum in the opening words of the Communist Manifesto that 'the history of all hitherto existing society is the history of class struggles'. At this level class becomes an analytic tool for the interpretation of the broader sweep of social history. At another level class is used as a means by which we predict the everyday behaviour of those whom we encounter: the reaction of an upper-class person to a given stimulus will differ from that of a lower-class person. In the latter mode classes can be seen as static entities; in the former they are undoubtedly dynamic.

Finally, as we have already noted, social class is not only a construct of scholars, but is a term used every day by the ordinary members of society. With it they individually and collectively assess their position in society, and perhaps seek to improve this. With it they judge the legitimacy of the systems of ranking within society, and either choose to operate within it or seek to change it. The scholars themselves, furthermore, are not mere observers of society; in publicising their analyses they help to shape the constructs used by those whom they study, and are themselves influenced by the interpretations of the latter.

Persuasive though the categorisation of a society in terms of social class undoubtedly is, however, it is not the only such mode. Members of a society may be ordered in terms of ethnic grouping, in terms of their past social origins and primordial loyalties rather than of their current social ranking. It is possible to imagine a society ethnically divided, in which the members of each group shared an identical pattern of social ranking; one would here assess the relative significance of relationships within ethnic groups and class. Alternatively, and here one can think of more examples in our present world, ethnic divisions are congruent with those of class: the whites, the members of the host community, are mostly at the top; the coloureds, the immigrants, are mostly at the bottom.

CLASS MODELS

Let us turn now to examine the varieties of model used in our constructs of social class.

The first major difference lies in the level of abstraction employed. People exist and events happen in the real world;

a model may be isomorphic with these or it may be concerned with principles of relationship. Thus classes may be seen as categories of individuals – everyone must be assigned to a class; or they may be seen as collectivities, visible in mass action in which the identity of individuals is lost. Propositions raised at this level can be empirically verified – do people with high incomes also have good education, mix with their social equals? Or, a rather more difficult proposition, do workers strike in certain conditions? Here we are already moving from the level of people to that of events – class is what happens. And with this move we pass from the actor's own explanations of his action to the unintended consequences noted by the observer; class becomes an observer's construct and the meanings assigned by the individual actor become less relevant in analysis. Further along the path to abstraction we find class used to define patterns of relationships. Class is thus concerned with the relationship between employer and employee, or, at another level, between capital and labour.

So just as the 'state' is used to designate at one level sets of individuals such as politicians, civil servants and the like, and at another level a pattern of relationships (Miliband, 1969), so 'class' has been variously used. Propositions raised at an abstract level are not capable of empirical verification. The acceptability of such structuralist formulations rests in their elegance and simplicity and perhaps in their ideological legitimacy. Thus we find, at the extreme, those Marxists who denigrate most stratification studies as 'bourgeois empiricism' whilst their own discussions of the forces of history lack, almost completely, any reference to research designed to substantiate their propositions.

In building models we create categories and define a relationship between them (see Ossowski, 1963). This is a universal human activity, and though members of one culture may prefer certain patterns to others it seems likely that, within any culture, modes of categorisation are common to all aspects of experience. Our categories, furthermore, are not static; we are engaged in a continual process of simplifying the world by reducing the number of categories – yet as we do so more discordant elements emerge to attract our attention and we adjust the boundaries of our units to ensure a better fit.

One simple model is the dichotomy *a* versus *not-a* – a twofold division based upon a single attribute. In class terminology this appears as the 'haves' versus 'have nots' division, however 'haves' may here be defined. The relationship between the two may be expressed as functional – both are necessary for the maintenance of society; or as conflicting – the 'have nots' seek to enjoy the privileges of the 'haves' who themselves resist this claim. At the abstract level 'capital' and 'labour' are opposed in a similar functional or conflicting relationship.

Another model is the linear scale, along which items are evenly or unevenly distributed. A convenient way of subdividing such a scale is into three parts: two ends and the middle. These parts may be equal in size or, especially if the distribution follows the pattern of a normal curve, the middle may be larger than the ends. The relationship between the parts here is functional (though there can be competition for position on the scale).

A third model common in our thinking is that of concentric circles, the successive rings denoting an ever-increasing distance from the centre.

Finally, our categorisation may be based upon discrete entities each of which is recognisably different from the other; but such entities need not be hierarchically ranked, nor need they be all-inclusive.

Examples of such models in our social class constructs quickly come to mind. The dichotomy can be illustrated by the Marxist division of capitalist society into two opposed classes, the bourgeoisie and the proletariat. The linear scale is exemplified at its crudest in income categories, the Registrar General's hierarchy of occupations, or, in a more sophisticated manner, by Warner's (1949) index of status characteristics. Though Warner's studies now receive scant respect in the academic world, the terminology which he used in his classification of society remains current. The concentric circle model is like that used by the individual taking an ego-oriented view of society. He is at the centre, immediately surrounded by people like him. Distant from him are those with whom he has little contact and whom he may see as deviant. Along the vertical axis the very rich are at the top and society's drop-outs are at the bottom, and along the horizontal axis can be found the members of other communities. Discrete entities are frequently portrayed in occupational terms – landlords, manufacturers, intelligentsia, workers, artisans, peasants, and so on; any two or more may be related in terms of function or conflict but a universal relationship may not exist. It is entities such as these that Marx used in his descriptions of nineteenth-century politics; the 'non-antagonistic classes' seen in contemporary socialist societies by their ideologues can be of this type too.

As we shall see later, an actor may use different models according to context. Strickon (1967) describes how the people in the Argentinian village he studied saw their national society in dichotomic terms: the oligarchy was seen as oppressing the masses whilst local society was seen as a number of interdependent occupational groups. Again, some elements may recur in more than one model; the us/them distinction is appropriate to the dichotomic and the concentric circle models, and perhaps also to groups on a linear scale.

In many recent studies attempts have been made to construct models of this kind from informants' replies to questionnaires, surveys, or interviews. A frequent charge is that such data can be manipulated to fit a variety of models – much depends on the manner in which the researcher interprets his material. Here I have constructed ideal types to which the models used both by scholars and actors tend to conform.

Our discussion so far has concerned the number of units employed in the categorisation of society and the relationships between them. We must now examine the criteria upon which the division is based. Three elements can be discussed in the familiar class constructs: a concern with production, a focus on consumption and the expression in political action of demands arising from these two.

Social inequality derives from unequal capacity to gain an income, whether this inequality is a result of innate ability or socially imposed discrimination. Descriptively, modern industrial society is divided between those who work with their hands, the manual or blue-collar workers, and those who work with their brains, the non-manual or white-collar workers. In terms of social relationships the division is between those who control production – ownership being only one form of control – and those who are controlled. The higher rewards of the non-manual workers are held to derive from the greater importance for society of their efforts. The controllers, on the other hand, exact a surplus from their workers, the mode of extraction varying with the technological level of production. Implicit in this control is the concept of power; some individuals are able to direct the lives of others. Thus the dominant class wields power, the subordinate class is subject to it.

Such stark dichotomous divisions in the production process are, however, modified by a number of further considerations. Some of these concern the individual response to subordination. On the one hand men and women have varying chances, either of improving their position within their own social class or of moving from one class to another. For some people the work situation offers little or no scope for advancement; the worker remains on the same grade throughout his or her life. Others are on a career ladder. The manual/non-manual distinction is not completely congruent with this difference, for the lack of career prospects is now found in routine clerical employment. In such social movement one's bargaining position (or market situation in the Weberian sense) depends on one's control of resources – capital, skills, patronage. On the other hand, the relationship between men engaged in production determines the degree to which they can act collectively to improve their position. Those who work together in a factory can combine more effectively than artisans working in their homes. Militancy may be higher in a big factory than in a smaller one. Clerical workers may be fragmented in their work situation, owing allegiances to many different bosses; on the factory floor large numbers may be controlled by a few foremen. The work experience generates interests – although these may not be similarly perceived by actor and observer. These are articulated as demands; and it is from such demands that relationships of conflict and competition emerge.

Earning a living is clearly prior in both time and importance to the spending of one's income. Yet a focus on consumption continues to be important in class constructs, for life-styles are more easily perceived than production relationships. It is assumed, with good reason, that individuals of similar social rank will intermarry, entertain each other informally, belong to the same voluntary associations, live in the same type of residential areas, send their children to the same schools. From this interaction will emerge social attitudes and behaviour which differentiate members of one class from another; indeed, if little intergenerational social mobility exists, distinct subcultures will develop.

In recent decades, however, the priority given by Marxists to productive relationships has won greater adherence; at the same time the significance of the actor's own understanding of his society has also been more strongly emphasised, and as a corollary the totality of his social life, his relationships at work, at home and in leisure activities, are increasingly stressed. Consumption issues also generate demands which find political expression, for example, prices, housing and education policies. These demands, together with those deriving from production relationships, are aggregated into the programmes of political parties. A limited number of parties can exist in the modern state, and it might be assumed that party membership reflects the class composition of society. This theme is, however, deferred until later in this chapter.

The models described above serve to limit the number of classes in a society: two in the case of dichotomy, perhaps three with linear scaling. But the criteria used in defining classes are so diverse that a multitude of classes is posited. Following Weber, three forms of ranking have been distinguished: economic class based on production criteria, social status groups based upon consumption criteria and life-styles, and political parties based upon action or the articulation of demands. But the essence of our class constructs is that there should be but one perceived mode of ranking; it is incongruous and impracticable to place an individual high on one scale, low on another.

There are two ways out of this difficulty. Either one can argue, as Runciman (1966) does, that although analytically distinct the three modes of grouping are for practical purposes usually congruent. The economically powerful are also rich and politically conservative. Or one can ignore one mode at the expense of the others. Thus Warner's social classes are in fact status groups, defined in terms of income, occupation, education and residence and substantiated by the subjective evaluation of members of the community. Production criteria are mentioned, but play an insignificant role in his constructs. Marx, on the other hand, stressed the production criteria, and his followers have even more dogmatically asserted the primacy of the economic domain. But as Giddens (1973, p. 105) has noted: 'The most important blank spots in the theory of class concern the processes whereby 'economic classes' became 'social classes', and whereby in turn the latter are related to other social forms.'

John Rex (1961, ch. 8) has neatly tried to combine the two schemata in suggesting that Warner's three top classes form the bourgeoisie and his three lower classes the pro-letariat, the divisions within the latter referring to social attitudes: those in the lower-middle class aspire to move upwards, those in the upper-lower class accept their position, those in the lower-lower class reject the dominant values of the society. But the problem of equating economic class with social status remains. Thus Wesolowski (1979), for example, in discussing the nature of the capitalist state, distinguishes between the economically dominant *class* of capitalists and the *strata* of bureaucrats, party politicians and ideologues who have their own specific interests and privileges, which may well coincide with those of the dominant class though they are not properly within it.

In our attempts to find patterned regularities we tend to oversimplify. The complexity of the world cannot be adequately represented by two or three categories. The number of instances increases in which individual units depart significantly from the mode of the category. In a dichotomy adjacent units on the side of the dividing line seem to have more in common than each has with units of the same category at the extremes of the range.

With the linear scale model the further subdivision of classes is relatively easy, as Warner has shown in dividing the upper, middle and lower classes into six units; by the same process he might have created nine classes! But a dichotomous division cannot be subdivided using the same criterion; as Parkin (1974a) has argued, in postulating a conflict relationship between dominant and subordinate classes, conflict cannot be used to differentiate categories within each class. He argues that conflict here does exist and leads to opposed social groups, those having privileges striving to be exclusive, those without them trying to achieve solidarity in opposing the privileges. But this procedure leads logically to the proliferation of groups and to individuals being members of both 'in' and 'out' groups; thus skilled craftsmen are members of a proletariat opposed to the capitalists, but are privileged in comparison with unskilled workers and strive to maintain this status. As in Dahrendorf's (1959) discussions of power and authority, a social process is described which is pertinent to social ranking but does not lead to the perception of classes. Parkin's difficulty would seem to stem from too loose a use of 'conflict', a term which covers many different relationships. More usefully, one might distinguish between the structural 'contradiction' between capital and labour, the 'conflict' between the classes derived from these abstractions and the 'competition' between individuals for specific privileges within each class.

Marx's vision of an increasing polarisation of the

bourgeoisie and proletariat with the relative or actual immis-
eration of the latter, backed by Disraeli's image of Britain's
'two nations', has been bedevilled by the development of the
relatively affluent 'middle class' and ultimately by the
suggested growth of homogeneity: 'We are all middle class
now.' The incompatibility of these two trends may be
resolved in assigning to the middle class those who occupy
ambiguous positions in the dichotomous model. Thus white-
collar wage-earners may be seen as exploited proletarians,
but a relatively high income and perquisites, good career
prospects and their position in the authority hierarchy
variously differentiate them from the true working class.

This model, in which the middle class occupies a marginal
or ambiguous position between two clearly defined polar
classes, is clearly different from that in which the middle
class comprises the majority of the population, upholding
the dominant norms and values which are flouted by the
small upper class or aristocracy or rejected by the lower
class or lumpenproletariat.

Poulantzas (1973a, 1973b) argues for a plurality of
classes within the basic dichotomous division of exploiters
and exploited, and he furthermore distinguishes strata,
which are broad social categories lacking cohesion, and
factions, which have economic interests and can act as
social forces. Both strata and factions exist within classes;
thus the labour aristocracy is a faction within the working
class. Members of particular social strata, such as bureaucrats, cut across classes: top bureaucrats are bourgeois,
lesser ones are petit bourgeois. Poulantzas distinguishes
furthermore between productive workers, the true working
class, and non-productive workers; for him the white-collar
clerks are the new petite bourgeoisie, contrasted in
economic relationships with a traditional artisan petite
bourgeoisie but sharing a similar political and ideological
outlook. Poulantzas's schema represents in part the
attempt to mediate the more abstract Marxist theorising
with the needs of the leaders of a highly successful and
powerful Communist Party to define its core support and
permissible allies.

These attempts to differentiate within classes exist within a static structure; a diachronic approach yields complexity of a different order. Marx presented a typically Victorian evolutionary sequence of societies: primitive – slave – feudal – capitalist – socialist. In each stage two classes were opposed, but relics of the classes appropriate to a previous stage lingered on, whilst nascent classes of the succeeding stage began to develop. Thus the traditional petite bourgeoisie would become proletarianised as independent craftsmen were forced into factory employment. Similarly evolutionary tendencies are posited in contemporary modernisation theories. One consequence of these theories has been the relatively small amount of attention paid by scholars to those groups which are supposedly disappearing; the focus is upon those which will be significant in the coming decades, the 'new working class', perhaps, of skilled technicians.

It is increasingly recognised, however, that societies do not change in this linear fashion but in a more complex manner. The apparent coexistence in Latin America of both capitalist and feudal modes of production has led Marxists to debate the stage to which this continent should be assigned in its colonial and immediately post-colonial periods (for example, Frank, 1969; Laclau, 1971). Looking, too, at the contemporary scene, it has become apparent that the informal sector of artisans and petty traders, of men and women bound by traditional relationships, is not withering away in the Third World cities. In fact the growth of shanty towns has accentuated its presence.

Scholars now see this so-called informal sector as a creation, at an abstract level, of the formal capitalist sector, and highly interdependent with it. In other words, subject to rates of foreign investment and such exogenous factors, the two will continue to coexist. In abstract terms this is depicted as the coexistence of two modes of production, one being a dominant mode, the other subordinate, within a single social formation. (These terms are not consistently used by the several authors sharing this approach.) Thus, as we shall see in the next chapter, the informal or petty commodity production sector is interdependent with, and subordinate to, the formal capitalist sector in Third World cities. But this model of the economy produces problems for our class constructs if each mode of production is assumed to have its opposed classes.

Classes persist through time, though not without change. In the dichotomous model the dynamism is provided by the relationships of conflict; the struggle produces continual shifts in the characteristics of each class. But it is usually assumed that membership of each class remains relatively static; studies of social mobility here have little relevance. In holding that social consciousness derives from present class position, Marxists even further deny the usefulness of mobility studies. On the other hand, the linear scale model readily presents the image of a ladder; classes, the 'rungs' as it were, remain static but people are continuously moving up or down. This image supports the view of a society with equality of opportunity, with considerable social homo-geneity and consensus regarding the dominant values. In contrast, the dichotomous model suggests the existence of separate sub-entities and dominant and subordinate deviant value-systems. These two models thus sustain rival ideologies which themselves reinforce specific perceptions of society.

Some social mobility exists, or is believed to exist, in almost all societies. The tales of peasants who become lords and of poor workers who become prosperous industrialists sustain the legitimacy of the class system. Studies of the amount of social mobility are, implicitly, ideologically motivated since, in showing whether a society is open or closed, they demonstrate the validity of the 'ladder' or con-flict models. Until recently these studies have been very crude, restricted to measurement of intergenerational movement across the non-manual/manual divide. Move-ment within each such class has largely been ignored. Recent studies, such as those of Goldthorpe (1980) and his colleagues, are far more sophisticated and give a much better picture of movement across the whole spectrum. Frequently these studies indicate a buffer zone, coinciding with the strata of lower non-manual workers and skilled workers, with their very similar incomes, life-styles and modes of wage employment, within which there is considerable intergenerational movement. Above and below this zone movement is less common. The cause of this movement has been attributed by Richardson (1977) to the retention by those mobile persons of their value orientations; thus those of 'middle-class' origin (in status terms) who become manual workers will endeavour to raise their children to the higher class; similarly the upwardly mobile manual workers will often fail to consolidate their position by adopting the values of the higher class, and their children will revert to their parents' earlier status. This manner of looking at class perception contrasts with that of earlier studies which stressed the psychological problems of adjustment for the mobile person.

Marxist interest in social mobility has been awakened by the rediscovery of the concept of social reproduction. In the 1950s Marxism was associated with change and conflict, Parsonian structuralism with stability and consensus, and with pattern maintenance. Now the Marxists, too, ask: 'Why do societies persist relatively unchanged?' In so doing they focus on both the impact of the dominant ideology and the lack of access to resources in the subordinate classes. Thus schools are seen as socialising children to dominant values (or alienating those which reject them); and thus, in spite of the overtly egalitarian nature of the state system, our schools stratify children into pre-existing patterns. Mobility studies have become relevant, though the distinction will always remain between those who hope to demonstrate respectively the openness, or the closed nature, of their societies.

CLASS PERCEPTIONS

Class constructs are used, as we have seen, not only by scholarly observers but also by the members of the observed society. Until recently most standard textbooks on social stratification have distinguished between objective class, which is that defined or measured by the scholar, and subjective class, which is the actor's self-evaluation. Survey respondents were asked in which of (usually) three classes they placed themselves; the discrepancy between their answers and the scholar's placement provided data for study. Respondents were rarely asked to what *extent* they used class concepts or *how* they saw their society divided. Rather they were accused of 'false consciousness' in deviating from the observer's own interpretation.

The swing towards an action-oriented or phenomenological sociology, deriving through several paths from Weber and even having Marxist adherents who claim its compatibility with the structural approaches of that school, has led to these very questions being posed (for example, Bulmer, 1975; Davis, 1979). Action is explained in terms of the actor's own understanding of the situation. This does not exclude the possibility that actors misuse concepts available to them, that they have little information, that either they are not very intelligent and so cannot process the information available to them, or the information is so complex that only a computer could process it; in all such situations the outcome might be very different from that originally intended by the actor. Nor does it deny that opportunities perceived by the actor, or the constraints acting upon him, are presented by the real world independently of his own volition. The observer, in making his own interpretation of a situation, includes both his assessment of the perceptions of individual actors and his predictions of their actions. His interpretation is the richer by this inclusion; but the elucidation of the actor's perceptions is no easy task.

The scholar presents to the world an interpretation judged by its simplicity, elegance and congruence. The actor rarely has to engage in such a task. He holds a variety of concepts and a range of propositions which relate to these concepts; these propositions are often incongruent with each other. These images are selected as appropriate to specific situations. In constructing the model apparently used by the actor the researcher must both interpret his responses and discriminate between them, an activity which draws us far from the actor's own images. The questions which are used prompt answers of a specific kind; terms may be used symbolically – thus some would argue that a distinction made between rich and poor implies not a consumption but a power model (see, for example, Moorhouse, 1976). The point to be stressed here, however, is that the models which we ascribe to the actors are of the same general pattern of those used by the scholars.

Earlier studies of such actors' models, classically exemplified by that of Goldthorpe *et al.* (1969), posited a single (or perhaps dominant) model for each actor. Workers were thus classified as traditional, deferential, or privatised according to their productive relationships *and*, which is more important, the model which they used in interpreting society. Some critics have claimed that, in practice, they have been unable to find these three kinds of workers – they must be 'ideal types'. Others, like myself, have argued that the individual actor has many models. As we have already noted, the Argentine villagers described by Strickon used one model for their national, another for their local, society. The actor may on occasion externalise himself from his society, becoming its observer, but most of the time he holds an ego-oriented view of the world around him. Each view may elicit different class constructs.

Such a focus on actor's models prompts the question 'whence do they derive?'. The actor responds to a given situation in terms of his interpretation of it, and this means in terms of concepts and propositions previously learned. These are generated both by the actor's own experiences, past and present, and by external influences such as his peers and the ideologies directed towards him. Thus the family in which the actor was originally socialised and his career experience, his social mobility, become important factors. So too are the peers with whom he discusses matters, his neighbours, members of his ethnic group, for they shape his attitudes. And equally important are the messages beamed to him daily by the news media. Thus whilst we may be concerned specifically with the actor at work, his interpretation and response to this situation will ultimately involve a study of his total relationships.

The view of society as discussed above should properly be termed 'social consciousness', for the actor may make little use of class constructs in interpreting his world. 'Class-consciousness' means consciousness of class, and as we have noted already this tends to mean class as defined by the scholar/observer. The term is certainly used thus by Marxists, although their elucidation of the meaning of the term falls incredibly far short of the importance attached to it. In effect they have used the term at an abstract level and empirical studies by non-Marxists, often casting doubt on the concept, have been derided by them.

Levels of class-consciousness have recently been defined by a number of scholars in relatively similar terms, in an attempt to elaborate Marx's distinction between a class in itself and a class for itself (for example, Miliband, 1971; Giddens, 1973; Mann, 1973). At the lowest level consciousness is manifest in members' awareness of their identity as a class. Next they are conscious of their specific interests, they struggle to promote these interests and increasingly come to understand the means by which their goals might be achieved. The 'highest' form of consciousness, revolutionary consciousness, is attained when workers see their struggle as constituting a (necessary) process of historical change. In the opinion of many there is a hierarchy of levels through which the working class is expected to progress; but for some revolution is dependent upon the working class attaining a high level of consciousness, while for others it is the first task of the revolution to create such consciousness. But, as Giddens has noted, the two forms of positive consciousness are not hierarchically ranked. Workers may be conscious of a conflict between their interests and those of their employer, they will strive for better wages and engage in the economistic activity labelled by Lenin 'trade union consciousness'. Again they may be aware of the structural contradiction between labour and capital and strive for revolutionary change. The former implies the acceptance of society as it is; the latter, a radical change in society. It would perhaps be unlikely that those who saw the contradictions in their society did not participate in the struggle for better immediate conditions; but the former form of consciousness which basically accepts society as it is does not necessarily develop from the latter. This debate is reflected in the policy discussions of politically radical groups. By some, reform is seen as detrimental to the quick achievement of revolution; as the worker's condition is ameliorated he ceases to struggle and the eventual crisis is postponed. Others, however, argue that the worker is entitled to seek current gains in addition to a problematic future paradise, and they assert in addition that striving for the former he is in fact educated for the latter task.

Class constructs are sterile if they are confined to the categorisation of individuals either by their attitudes or by their beliefs. Classes are manifest in action. But to pass from the actors' models to their actions raises difficult methodological and philosophical problems. Questionnaire responses, divorced from any reference to specific situations, are unreliable predictors of behaviour. On the other hand, the tendency of an observer to interpret action according to his own concepts rather than according to those of the actor can be dangerous. For instance, to an observer strikes may look the same in London, Lagos and Lima, but are they seen in similar fashion by workers in those three cities? The importance of an understanding of the actor's perceptions of his situation must, however, override the difficulties encountered in elucidating it.

The scholarly observer is usually content to describe the world as he sees it; *qua* scholar he proffers no value judgements. The actor is not so constrained; he views the world both as it is and as it might be. That is, he questions the legitimacy of his society. Acceptance or rejection may be viewed both positively and negatively. The actor may see the structure of his society as legitimate, subscribing to its dominant ideology; he may positively try to exploit the opportunities inherent in the structure to improve his own position, becoming socially mobile; or he may negatively accept his position. Similarly, in rejecting his society he may positively strive for the creation of an alternative society; or he may opt out, becoming a 'drop-out'. In making these distinctions an important factor is the knowledge and resources available to the actor. The very poor are usually too ignorant to be able to formulate an image of an alternative society; they merely see what is wrong with the present one. Again, an actor may hold an image of an alternative society but feel that resources available to those striving for it are insufficient for that image to become reality. One response to this is to strive even harder; another is to become apathetic.

Action may take a variety of forms. It may be manifest as tension, unstructured expressions of discontent lacking coherent or clearly expressed goals. A high level of activity purposively directed towards specific goals may be termed militancy. But not all tension and militancy is class action; the focus of action may be directed elsewhere, to ethnic interests, for instance. Once again, however, we must be aware of the distinction between the actors' perceptions of their interests and goals and the observers' interpretations of the outcomes of action.

The articulation of numerous and diverse interests becomes effective only when these become aggregated into the programmes of political parties. Marxists have always recognised the importance of the party, and the fact that countless instances of spontaneous protest do not make a revolution. (From here they are led to debate the respective roles of the working class and of the middle-class intellectual leadership.) But many Marxists are now critical of the crude subordination of the political to the economic sphere and argue for a relative autonomy of the political. Parties develop in specific historical circumstances and the logic of their development is substantially independent of economic or social change.

At the more abstract level a succession of political events may be interpreted by an observer as a progressive movement; this progression may not have been apparent to the individual actors, and the interpretation of it as such may indeed be ascribed to the observer's wishful thinking. Thus Clark (1978) has challenged the view that a series of agrarian protests in nineteenth-century Ireland constituted the intensification of the rural class struggle; as he shows, the protests involved very different interest groups and were about different issues. It is in such situations that statements about class-consciousness or the class struggle become ideological weapons rather than empirically testable propositions about the real world.

In this chapter I have outlined some of the principal differences in class constructs in contemporary use. The items listed will serve as a framework or checklist with which to describe in the following chapters the characteristics of the urban poor in the Third World cities. I have not made a comparative evaluation of the various models, since such an evaluation must be in terms of specific data. I only ask, does the model provide us with a satisfying explanation of the world about us? The constructs described are those which have been developed in the study of Western industrial society; it is not my task to describe this society but to assess the applicability of the constructs developed in this context to another very different one.

In conclusion, let me reiterate the dialectical relationship between the real world and the constructs which we employ in understanding it. In a large measure the problems which we identify are the product of the models we use. Thus we are conscious of substantial changes in the working class in Western society: it is materially more affluent than at the turn of the century; the mass media are more pervasive. The working class seems to be assuming the styles of life and the ideology of the middle class, to be becoming middle class. Yet exploitation is still seen to exist; a clear divide between middle- and working-class attitudes is demonstrated. Industrial strife is less violent, but is it less militant? Such differences sustain the rival models which, in their turn, focus attention upon certain characteristics.

Similarly, in predicting future change, we try to identify the groups or categories within the working class which will play the most significant roles. Rival candidates are: the traditional working class, the manual workers in industry who represent a numerically declining category in modern industrial society; the 'new working class' of skilled technicians and junior non-manual executives; the under class or marginals, the very poor and often immigrant workers.

The Third World presents different phenomena; but the basic questions which we ask are nevertheless similar.

3

Economic Categories

The impact of the Western world upon the peoples of the Third World may be viewed in countless ways. Here we are concerned with the growth of wage labour and an urban workforce; these are related but not congruent concepts.

From the initial impact of the sixteenth-century voyages of discovery to the present day, the political scene has changed dramatically and in diverse ways. The Spanish and Portuguese colonies of Latin America gained their independence, with the power being passed to an entrenched creole elite, long before the African peoples lost theirs. Yet in recent decades economic changes within Third World states have followed a substantially uniform pattern – a pattern determined more by changes in the economic structure of the industrial West than by local developments in the poorer countries (Lloyd, 1967; Gilbert, 1974; Markovitz, 1977; B. Roberts, 1978).

In the centuries before the Second World War the economies of the Third World nations were at first dominated (apart from their subsistence production) by the export of luxuries, and then, as the industrial revolution in the West got under way, of raw materials. To a small extent the production of exported commodities was in the hands of the indigenous peasantry, the cocoa and groundnut farmers or oil-palm harvesters of West Africa, the coffee farmers of East Africa, for instance. Most exported commodities, however, came from estates and plantations, from mines owned and operated by entrepreneurs of foreign origin, many of whom subsequently settled to form a locally dominant group. These enterprises relied upon a labour force which was to some extent permanent, to some extent migratory (see, for example, Laite, 1981). On the agricultural estates men worked perhaps as share-croppers or, as on the haciendas of Latin America where peasants performed tasks both on the land and in the house, in other highly paternalistic forms of relationship. In the mines forced labour was sometimes used, as in the *mita* system of Peru. Or alternatively migrants supplied a steady stream of unskilled labour, coming perhaps as 'target' workers and staying for several months before returning to their rural homes. Open-cast tin mines in Nigeria were able to operate successfully with a rapid turnover of seasonal migrants who came for only a few weeks during their slack agricultural season.

These enterprises constituted an 'enclave' economy producing little effect upon the indigenous economy. The 'trickle down' effect was more marked with peasant production, giving rise to new groups of traders and craftsmen, but an accumulation of capital sufficient to generate a local industrialisation was not possible either at the local level or at the national level where the indigenous bourgeoisie has been more committed to the commercial export of agricultural products and minerals. Manufacturing industry made a slow start in Latin America at the beginning of the twentieth century, its progress in each country being conditioned by the vagaries of the market for exported commodities and the interests and initiative of local businessmen. In tropical Africa manufacturing industry, save for the occasional brewery, was non-existent before 1945.

In this situation the capital cities remained small, seats of government and in many cases ports. A substantial category of artisans, petty traders and domestics served the dominant groups and the clerical workers. The development of an infrastructure to serve the export economy, of roads, railways, power and harbours, necessitated both a small force of relatively skilled men (particularly in railways) and a large force of unskilled and often migrant men (as in road or railway building), a force which was not necessarily located in the capital cities.

In the past three decades a number of factors have

interacted to produce both a marked acceleration and a radical change in the direction of development. The colonial states of Africa and Asia have gained political independence; and here, as in South America, parliamentary democracy has spurred on the provision of social services such as health and education to the masses. The belief of local leaders that successful development lies in the development of import-substituting manufactures has coincided with the discovery by foreign companies that profits are possible through investment in such industries. The location both of bureaucracies and of manufacturing industry in the metropolitan cities has triggered an urban immigration far in excess of the wage employment formally created.

Let me elaborate some of these points. A very large proportion of the industrial development of the Third World has been financed from abroad. In establishing their subsidiaries in the Third World cities, international companies have usually favoured capital-intensive production; relatively few workers are employed even though low wages are one of the many attractions of the locale. The wages paid, however, though low by Western standards, are often high relative to other income opportunities in the city, and such comparatively high wages stimulate migration. These industries usually serve a middle- and upper-strata market and do little to increase its size; with the notable exceptions of such countries as South Korea, Taiwan, Hong Kong and perhaps Brazil, no export market has been created; often local tariffs and protection costs serve to raise the prices of products. Most of the components used in these foreign-financed industries are imported from abroad; few are produced locally. The industries are reliant too on the research and technological development of the parent companies; few opportunities are created for local initiative. In sum, it is argued that the dominance of these foreign companies has stultified the local internal development of the economy. The contribution of these industries to the gross national product is high, but their contribution to the creation of employment is low (for Kenya see, for example, Kitching, 1977, 1980; Swainson, 1977).

A second characteristic of Third World economies is the control of the state. The major utilities tend to be in public ownership. The state has been active in establishing certain new industries in fields which the foreign investor has been reluctant to enter. It has nationalised existing foreign-owned enterprises, either for its own assumed economic advantage, or as a measure to win popular support. The size of highly centralised service bureaucracies, demonstrated by the number of new ministerial office blocks in the cities and of its police and armed forces, is commensurate with that of industrial nations in the mid-twentieth century – and not of those nations a century earlier when their own industries were slowly developing.

A third feature is the population explosion in the cities, which have been growing at rates often exceeding 5 per cent a year (Eames and Goode, 1973; B. Roberts, 1978; Lloyd, 1979). In the rural areas there has been little investment in peasant agriculture; land reform measures, the capitalisation of estates, an increasing birth rate, the replacement of labour-intensive by mechanised road building, have all in various ways limited opportunities for rural employment. In contrast the cities seem to provide opportunities not only for immediate employment but also, and this is more important, for career advancement to positions rarely available in the rural areas. But the number of people who seek wage employment each year in industry or public service, including both recent immigrants and the offspring of a young city population, greatly exceeds the number of jobs created. Overseas emigration, the outlet for the surplus population of the industrialising states of nineteenth-century Europe, is a feature of relatively few Third World countries. No public social security exists for these surplus people, and whilst they exploit such niches as they find in the economy to gain a meagre and often precarious income, they also maintain close links with kinsmen, compatriots and their home rural area in order to achieve a measure of security. A few do become fairly successful small entrepreneurs, but dominant in the image of the Third World city is the stark contrast between the modern office blocks, the landscaped industrial estates, the supermarkets and residential suburbs of the affluent, and the shanty towns and inner city slums, home of the artisan, the petty trader and the unskilled worker.

This pattern of development has produced a class structure which differs significantly from that of Western industrial countries. Descriptively, the following categories emerge.

The dominant groups within the Third World nations have very little control over the economy. At the upper level it is mainly in foreign ownership; at the lower level it is in the hands of the artisans and peasant farmers. In many states where a landed oligarchy once held supreme political power groups oriented more towards industry and finance have now gained control. The political elite of decision-makers, be they elected politicians, senior civil servants, or officers of the armed forces, are salary-earners; their control of foreign enterprises constitutes a negotiated dependency. From the exercise of their duties they derive perquisites which increase their wealth and enable them to participate both in major industry through shareholding and in petty entrepreneurial activities such as property ownership, farming, or trading. A more immediate control of business is exercised by an expatriate population, having no direct voice in local politics, and by local people in managerial posts – posts which usually keep them removed from the highest levels of policy-making. Indigenously owned businesses tend to be relatively few and small; some are clearly allied to foreign firms, being virtual subsidiaries, others are in competition with them and promote a more nationalistic approach to economic development. Serving both the public sector and, to a greater extent, industry and commerce, are the professionals such as architects, accountants, lawyers, and the like.

In tropical Africa these dominant groups have emerged in recent decades from the indigenous society, the move from a poor rural home to a high office often being achieved within a single generation (Lloyd, 1966). At the other extreme the Latin American dominant groups are largely descended from immigrants from Europe within the past century; they are still predominantly 'white' though in certain circumstances and situations *mestizos* have reached the top echelons of society (Lipset and Solari, 1967).

Below these dominant groups are the intermediate strata of clerks and middle-professionals and executives, and of the more successful indigenous entrepreneurs. Individuals here are variously upwardly and downwardly mobile. In the Third World the social distinction between manual and non-manual workers remains striking. However low their relative remuneration, clerks and teachers usually possess tangible educational qualifications and see themselves as being on the lower rungs of a career ladder up which they aspire to climb, through further training or patronage.

The urban workers, to be discussed more fully later in this chapter, can be divided into three groups: first the wage employees in the larger industrial and commercial companies; secondly, those in the public sector; thirdly, those in the informal sector, whether as self-employed persons or as apprentices, journeymen, or wage labour in family concerns. In looking at the distribution of these workers in the Third World city one notices the high proportion of them in government, as opposed to private, employment. The proportion of people engaged in manufacturing is small compared with the numbers in the service sector, the relative size of which is again commensurate with that of contemporary advanced industrial nations. Indeed, official figures relating to the numbers of persons engaged in manufacturing can be misleading; a factory producing goods for popular consumption, a brewery, for instance, may employ relatively few people in the production process, but many as drivers and clerks in distribution; again, census figures for the population engaged in manufacturing often include both factory operatives and artisans, the latter frequently outnumbering the former.

A conceptualisation of these groups and categories as

social classes depends to a large extent on one's view of the development process. Two rival approaches compete (Roxborough, 1979). The one assumes that the poorer nations are following the same path as that taken by the industrial nations in becoming 'modernised' from a 'traditional past; ultimately they will display the same features of class structure. Modernisation theory, however, focuses more upon the obstacles to change, such as attitudes which produce stagnation, than upon the emergent structures. In contrast is the view that the relationship between rich and poor nations is such that the latter will never catch up, indeed the gap may widen; the structures of their societies will be unlike those of the rich nations. Latin American theorists, in attempting to explain the failure of their nations' attempts to industrialise, developed the concept of dependency with its opposition between core and periphery. The concept, originally distinguishing Western industrial from Third World nations, has more recently been used to delineate sectors within the nation; but when translated into an opposition between city and rural hinterland it obscures or negates class divisions.

Two problems emerge from dependency theories. One, which is not the concern of this book, is the nature of the dominant groups. Are they a national or *comprador* bourgeoisie? Are they in fact a bourgeoisie at all, since their control over the economy is so tangential? (Frank, 1972).

The other problem, with which we *are* concerned, relates to the categorisation of the urban workers. The wage-earners in large industrial and commercial enterprises and in the public services can be termed a working class in that their relationships are similar to those in industrial nations. However, their social characteristics may differ – and in particular a continuing attachment to their rural homes may earn them the categorisation of a proto-proletariat; the true proletarian is fully committed to urban life and work.

A designation of the workers in the informal sector depends on one's predictions for their future. If one foresees substantial investment, albeit within the relations of dependency, so that new industrial enterprises drive out the independent artisan, the latter will be forced into factory employment; he, too, is thus at present only a proto-proletarian, being merely on the way to full membership of the proletariat. If, however, one predicts that the relative size of the informal sector will continue – the absorption of some members into wage employment or petty entrepreneurship being balanced by the inflow of new recruits, whether city-born or migrants – then such urban workers cannot be a proto-proletariat. However, they may be seen as occupying a very subordinate place in the economy and as being exploited by the dominant groups, whatever relationships of dependency and exploitation may exist within any particular little enterprise. To emphasise this subordination they again are termed proto-proletarian, yet policies designed to stimulate the small-scale entrepreneurs, as suggested by the ILO (1972) report on Kenya (criticised by Leys, 1973), obviously view them as an incipient petite bourgeoisie.

It is to such themes that we now turn for a more detailed analysis.

WAGE EMPLOYMENT

In general terms the relationship between wage-earner and employer is, in the large companies and public corporations, identical in Western industrial and Third World nations (Gutkind *et al.*, 1978). In the latter, however, the range of the conditions of employment between the large foreign firms and the indigenously owned businesses is, in most states, wider than in the West. It is this range, and the special characteristics attaching to each level, that we must now explore (see, for example, Peil, 1972).

At one extreme are the privileged strata of workers employed by the large, wealthy, multinational companies. These workers have been described as a 'labour aristocracy' although this term has been strongly criticised, as we shall see in the final chapter. Here let us examine the privileges which these workers do enjoy.

The foreign firm is usually anxious to present an

'acceptable face' of capitalism. Its managers have had to bargain with the political leadership of the Third World country for permission to establish there and for a variety of favours, tax concessions, and the like. It is vulnerable in that it can be used as a scapegoat for national ills and misfortunes. The indigenous government can apply a number of sanctions, some merely irritating, others much more serious, even though the basic principle of foreign investment is maintained. Such firms try to preserve a good popular image. In Nigeria it was customary, on the opening of a new factory, to place a large centre-page advertisement in the press proclaiming the size of the investment and the benefits accruing to the country; in smaller type the number of workers to be employed was given.

Wages in these firms are good, that is to say, they are generally higher than in other forms of available employment. In as much as the wage bill often constitutes only a small proportion of the cost of the final product, the management may accede readily to moderate demands for increases; if the product is for popular consumption and if the firm is one of very few suppliers, increasing costs are easily passed to the consumer. A stoppage of work will disrupt the flow of the financial return on capital investment and so managements are motivated to avoid strikes, but this does not mean that all employees are highly paid. In such factories a few highly skilled workers are necessary to service the machinery, but the majority are often engaged in dull and routine tasks with semi-automated machines, jobs which require little basic skill and a minimum of training. Such workers receive little or nothing more than the nationally established minimum wage.

At this point one must emphasise the poverty attaching to such a minimum wage. As national commissions of inquiry so often demonstrate, it is frequently only half of what is deemed necessary to maintain a man with a wife and children. Again one may compare this wage with the income expected by an established self-employed artisan or petty trader; often the latter is better off. The data of Balan *et al.* (1973) from Monterrey, Mexico, corroborated by those of

Peace (1979) from Agege, Nigeria, show that the income range in the informal sector tends to span that of wage-earners.

Working conditions are good. The factories are modern, often sited in landscaped industrial estates; high standards of cleanliness and hygiene are maintained. The firms tend to be scrupulous in adhering to the local labour code – a code which, being directed at such firms, imposes standards usual in the West today but far more exacting than anything known in the nineteenth century. Regular holidays are given; clinics are available for workers and their families; pension schemes, either those of the firm or the state, may provide basic social security and retirement benefits.

These firms prefer a stable labour force, although they may well have a casual labour sector. The permanent workers appreciate their position. Labour turnover is thus relatively low; indeed, as Wells and Warmington (1962) show in their comparison between the multinational ply-wood factory in Sapele in southern Nigeria and the Lebanese-owned groundnut-crushing mills of Kano in the north, turnover in the former was low even by contemporary English standards.

But the workers in these factories are the most exploited, using this term to denote the difference between their wage and the value added to the product by their labour. The degree of exploitation is furthermore visible to the worker as he sees the affluence in which the management, both expatriate and indigenous, live; through the investigations of his union officials he may, too, be dimly aware of the profits being repatriated.

In contrast to these privileged workers are those employed in other companies and in the public sector. Characteristic of the former are firms owned by Levantines or Asians and the indigenously owned company which has developed perhaps from an artisanal base. These tend to be smaller and more labour-intensive, a characteristic associated with both the form of ownership and the nature of the industry; textile and food-processing factories are prominent in this category. Wages tend to be lower and working conditions are usually markedly inferior. More frequent attempts are made to infringe the labour code by both legitimate and illegitimate means. For example, in several Latin American countries the code gives the permanently established worker very strong safeguards against arbitrary dismissal or even redundancy. In consequence firms (and some of the foreign firms described above adopt this practice too) will employ a man at the casual rate for twenty-nine days, then dismiss him to avoid making him an established worker, but re-employ him at the casual rate after a day or two. The worker may spend months or years in serving such an apprenticeship and waiting to be selected for permanent employment. The small indigenous entrepreneur is often unable to abide by the provisions of the labour code in giving security to his workers, in coping with the paperwork involved and in tax deduction. Rather than increase his enterprise to the size covered by the code, variously five, ten or perhaps twenty workers, he reverts to the 'putting out' system; in fact he turns back the clock of the industrial revolution.

Casual work is an even more dominant feature of the construction industry, one of the major employers of unskilled migrant labour. Here the large companies hire workers for the term of a specific building contract, dismissing all of them, except for a core of maintenance and managerial staff, as one project ends and re-employing them perhaps when another begins.

In the state sector one again meets relatively secure forms of employment with adequate conditions of work. But whilst the state employs a very high proportion of the clerks in the intermediate strata, it also employs a vast army of unskilled labourers as road-sweepers, office messengers and cleaners, and the like. Such workers receive that national minimum wage. But such is the government's wage bill, a bill that it can meet only from tax revenues, that the level of the minimum wage is kept to its lowest, and raised only by the strongest pressure from the workers or by evidence of inflation.

Such differences in conditions of employment might be

held to result from the degree of trade union organisation in the different sectors. Differences in the trade unions there certainly are, and they do seem to parallel those in the working conditions; but as the debate about the relationship between wage levels and union activity shows, in Africa at least it is difficult to identify the causal factor (for the final shots in the debate see R. Cohen *et al.*, 1971).

In the earliest instances of wage employment it is easy to find examples of workers who have bonded themselves together to protest, often successfully, against low wages or victimisation. But histories of the genesis of a trade union movement in Third World countries stress the efforts made by a country's political leaders to develop and channel union organisation along a 'responsible' path. Landsberger (1967) argues that in Latin American countries the politicians sought 'to capture labour's awakening political power'. In British colonial Africa in the years following 1945 officials were seconded to the labour departments with the specific task of stimulating the further formation of trade unions. This could be interpreted as an act of faith by a British Labour government, or as an attempt to deflect the workers from supporting the radical nationalist movements by pushing them into wage bargaining with individual employers.

Before these government-sponsored attempts to foster trade union growth, however, workers in certain occupational spheres were well organised. Among the earliest unions to be founded have been those of dockers, railwaymen and miners (Sandbrook and Cohen, 1975). Here the employer has usually been the government or a foreign company. Numbers of workers are large and often concentrated on a small work area. Grillo (1973, 1974) attributes the strength of the Uganda railway workers' union in part to the ability of a scattered workforce to communicate easily through those employees, drivers and guards, who travel on the trains. Another factor is the relatively high levels of skills possessed by such workers (migrant mine labour is here excepted), and the permanence of their employment. White-collar workers, too, have been well organised from an early period, notably teachers and clerks. Here their education has been an important factor, together with the income disparity which separates them from the higher professional strata. In Peru, for instance, schoolteachers are almost as poorly paid as skilled workers, a situation incongruous with their aspirations. Such countries have long experienced the frustrations expressed by lower white-collar workers who, in Western industrial countries, have only recently been demoted to the income level of the average manual worker.

As in the West, such trade unions can be politically powerful. Miners can halt production of their country's main export commodity and revenue-earner. Railwaymen can halt the flow of goods in the capitalist sector. Success encourages continuing and increasing militancy.

In the foreign manufacturing and commercial companies in many Third World states house unions are the rule; less frequently does one find craft unions. There are several reasons for this. Government assistance in union formation has worked through such companies. The variety of enterprises in a single city or industrial estate can militate against the perception of overlapping interests. Sometimes the unions have developed from consultative committees established within a more paternalistic framework. In such unions the interests of white- and blue-collar workers are often juxtaposed: workers of the former grade may tend to occupy leadership offices, though as Peace (1979) shows for Agege this need not be the rule. There is, of course, a strong consequent focus upon company matters rather than upon wider political issues. Such unions, furthermore, do not have the same political leverage as those of the big public corporations.

The larger foreign firms, especially those with international reputations, tend to have strong and effective unions. At the other extreme are firms owned, in many cases, by indigenous or Lebanese and Asian businessmen. Among some of these a strong hostility to union organisation exists, and any worker who shows signs of militancy in organising protest activity is quickly dismissed. The government itself may abet such practices in adjudicating the legality of the grounds of dismissal; it may even in situations of extreme tension encourage such action in victimising militant leaders whilst upholding the principles of trade union organisation. In the smaller enterprises a benignly paternalistic management obviates union formation; highly personal ties bind employer and worker, often expressed in kinship idioms and perhaps continuing from one generation to the next.

Among the mass of casual workers, those who are seeking permanent employment but are fired and rehired at monthly intervals, the daily-paid labourers in the public sector and the construction workers, union membership is non-existent or at best nominal. Such workers can demonstrate in protest against their employers but their bargaining powers are minimal; if they cease work there are scores of people anxious to replace them.

In Third World countries we must distinguish trade union activity at two levels: the national or federal, and the grass-roots or company levels. Most countries have a central trade union federations but literature on all three continents has stressed the hostility which often exists between the federations and the local constituent unions (Payne, 1965; Davies, 1966; R. Cohen, 1974). The former are often staffed by men who have not risen from the ranks of the workforce but who are educated, and seek a career in a bureaucratic hierarchy. It is alleged by the workers that their interests lie in their own careers and in perquisites such as foreign tours offered by international trade union bodies; corruption, frequently proved, is believed to exist even more widely. Again the federations, as we shall see in a later chapter, may either be co-opted by government into the single-party machine, vigorously opposed by government, or wooed by political parties. In each situation the workers see their demands as being poorly represented by the federation. Too often the latter, instead of taking the initiative in seeking reform or radical change, merely intervenes in spontaneous local protest in order to enhance its own image.

In this situation the individual trade unions are engaged mainly in 'economistic' issues, in bargaining about wages and work conditions. Here they may be quite effective and indeed can be highly militant, as instanced not only by strikes or threats of stoppage but also, as Peace (1974, 1979) demonstrates, by verbal activity, such as abuse of the bosses and recapitulation of stories of past unrest and protest. The trade union federations have, in general, failed both to co-ordinate these activities and to situate them in a framework of political analysis through which the more radical class-consciousness of the workers might be developed (good studies of trade unions include Friedland, 1969; Sulmont, 1975; Sengupta, 1978).

THE INFORMAL SECTOR

The striking overt difference between the worker in the modern foreign-owned factory and the back-street artisan has already been noted. For a long time development economists focused upon the activities of the former and largely ignored the latter, seeing him as contributing little or nothing to efforts to raise the gross national product. It was anthropologists who contrasted the two sectors, giving equal weight to each. Geertz (1963) distinguished the 'bazaar' from the 'firm', the former characterising the low-income, low-productivity sector and the latter the modern capitalist company. Later Hart (1973) coined the term 'informal economy' in describing the manner in which migrants to Accra, Ghana, find self-employment. More recently Marxists have reintroduced the concept of petty commodity production (see Foster-Carter, 1978).

The earlier distinctions derived from the traditional/modern dichotomy, seeing the firm as a foreign import whilst the bazaar was an adaptation of the peasant economy. Emphasis was thus placed upon the autonomy of the two systems. Increasingly, however, the relationships between the two have been stressed; thus the petty commodity mode of production is seen as existing only in subordination to the capitalist mode (Gerry, 1974; Le Brun and

Gerry, 1975; Moser, 1976; Bromley and Gerry, 1979; Santos, 1979).

With the growing popularity of the terms informal sector and economy, as they were used by analysts and planners, their lack of precision became increasingly evident. As each writer referred to certain characteristics germane to his own point of view, so the list of attributes lengthened. Enterprises in the informal sector are small family businesses, lack permanent buildings, have irregular hours of work, lack credit facilities, are unenumerated, employ the less literate workers, have a low productivity, have a low technological level, and so on. In sum these attributes provide quite a graphic description and yet no single enterprise shares all attributes and no single criterion is an adequate base for classification. The term is increasingly seen to be descriptive, but not of analytical use – and it is in the former manner that it is used here. 'Petty commodity sector' is a little more precise, but used strictly to denote producers of commodities it omits the providers of services; and in most cities traders outnumber artisans. Used loosely as a synonym of informal sector, it shares the lack of precision of the latter though it does benefit in emphasising the subordinate position of the sector.

The variety of activities performed within the informal sector is great and we must try to distinguish between them. We shall look successively at the structural position of these enterprises in the total economy and at their pattern of internal organisation.

The informal sector produces both goods and services. The artisan probably obtains his tools from the formal sector, rather than from other informal sector artisans; thus the tailor buys an imported sewing machine but the carver of tourist art may use tools made by the local blacksmith. Again the raw materials used by the artisan, cloth for the tailor or gold for the jeweller, are probably imported; furniture-makers may use wood cut by local timber merchants. The artisan may be producing components for use within a factory, working on a subcontractual arrangement; such a relationship has been described as prevalent in

Calcutta (where there are perhaps more indigenously owned factories) but it seems relatively rare in Africa (Bose, 1974). More usually the artisan is producing goods for consumption, either high-quality goods for the rich or cheap products for the poor. These may be made directly to the order of a client, they may be sold in the open market, sold to a shop again on a contractual basis, or sold to a middleman trader who disposes of them. In examining such activities we may see the nature of the linkages between the informal sector enterprise and other sectors of the economy. In so doing we see too how the artisan, although perceiving himself as an independent self-employed man, is in fact highly dependent, with respect both to his supply of tools and raw materials and to the marketing of his product.

In the same way we may classify the activities of those providing services. Repairers of motor vehicles, or electrical equipment, serve the more affluent and rely on the major firms for the supply of parts; many masons and painters work for a poor clientele. Traders obtain their imported wares from wholesalers and their foodstuffs from the central market or, more rarely, from the peasant producer. They sell from open market stalls or make regular visits to an established clientele. Among those providing personal services we may distinguish: the living-in domestic servant, paid a wage and given free board and lodging (a category included within the informal sector by default); the domestic living at home who provides services for a series of clients, for example, gardeners and launderers who work a day or a half-day in a succession of houses; letter-writers, midwives, undertakers and others who provide services to a personal clientele on an *ad hoc* basis; and taxi-drivers plying for hire in the city streets. Here too we may separate those who serve the rich from those who serve the poor.

Having established the various linkages existing in each such enterprise, our next task is to evaluate the degree of subordination. This may be either direct – by exploiting wealth flows in one direction, someone is accumulating at someone else's expense; or structured – the informal sector enterprise carries out functions which are necessary to the continued working of the formal sector enterprises.

Artisans working for middlemen who supply raw materials and market the product, or who work under subcontractual agreements, are, in effect, in a position little different from wage employees in the factory: their surplus is appropriated. Living-in domestics, by general agreement one of the most exploited of categories, enable their employers to undertake other highly remunerated jobs or to fulfil more adequately the social expectations of their high status. Other artisans and traders help to increase the profits of their suppliers whilst they accumulate at the expense of their customers, be they rich or poor. There is clearly a highly complex flow of wealth within the informal sector, that is to say, among the urban poor; yet it seems probable that on balance the flow from informal to formal sector is greater than that in the reverse direction.

Most of the activities in the informal sector are directed towards the more affluent strata; but some are oriented towards the poor, such as the making of sandals from old tyres for those who cannot afford proper shoes, the trading of goods in minute quantities and on credit. By enabling the poor to buy cheaply the informal sector, it is argued, helps to reduce wage levels in the formal sector. The poor may nevertheless be paying dearly for the commodities or services supplied; cigarettes purchased singly cost more than a whole packet, rice bought by the small tin is more expensive than the supermarket price for a 5-kilo bag. These services are such that the highly capitalised firm could not usually provide them, given its mode of operations; the small profits of the petty trader and artisan give them an advantage over the large company with wage employees. Yet as soon as an opportunity is presented for mass production, whether of low-quality goods for the poor or of high-quality goods for the rich, the big firms will exploit it. And it will probably be the school leavers who find jobs in the new companies, not the displaced artisans and traders who cling tenaciously to their declining share of the market until they are forced into casual labour or back to their villages.

We must now turn to the internal organisation of the informal sector enterprise. Studies emphasise the relative ease of entry. Levels of education tend to be low; big foreign companies and public bodies often demand a full primary education even though this may have little relevance for the tasks required, so the person with an incomplete schooling is excluded. The necessary skills are gained through apprenticeship. A fairly small capital outlay is needed to buy tools or initial stock. Entry to these trades and crafts was probably easier a decade or more ago than it is now. The market is becoming saturated, and those who retire may pass their trading site or clientele to a kinsman or compatriot.

The informal sector worker owns his tools, decides his strategy (within the constraints of the overall economy) and arranges the timing of his activities; he is in this sense his own master. Expansion of his business may take a variety of forms, the breadth of choice available often depending on the nature of the activity. He may involve his family in his work, paying them no direct remuneration. Whilst he goes to the central market to buy produce, a child runs the shop and his wife hawks through the streets; he sells, from an evening stall, food cooked by his wife during the day. Alternatively, he may insist that his children's schooling is of prior importance, hoping for a better career for them. Or he may see in the variety of occupations of household members a form of security against the unemployment or failure of any one person. To increase his labour force he may take apprentices, charging a fee reflecting his expenditure on their food and lodging and his profit from the services performed by them. On completion of training the apprentice may become a journeyman, perhaps owning some of his own tools and receiving a higher wage in consequence; the journeyman or wage employee may be allowed to use his master's equipment after hours for his own purposes. The possible arrangements are legion. But all the time the master works alongside his co-workers; the significant breaks come when he becomes an administrator or manager and, in social terms, when he ceases to 'live above the shop'.

The opportunities for the artisan or trader to accumulate capital depend on a number of factors. Early in the life-cycle the young man, unmarried or newly married, can save; later his children involve heavy expenditure until, at adolescence, they become income-earners and contribute to the household budget. Family labour and apprenticeship are unpaid; journeymen and employees tend to receive extremely low wages, which they tolerate in the hope that their master will eventually help them to establish their own enterprises. The profits accumulated in a single enterprise may either be reinvested in that business or in a wider range of activities, in schooling for children, in house-building, and the like. In the former case a limit to expansion may be the worker's lack of technological knowledge (he cannot use more expensive machinery) or managerial skills; the owner of a small fleet of taxis may prefer to give an old vehicle to one of his drivers to enable him to start on his own, the immediate loss of profit being compensated for by the increase in social prestige. Little credit is offered to persons in the informal sector by either commercial banks or government loan agencies. The petty entrepreneur finds it difficult to produce an adequate application, to provide security, or to promise regular repayment; and indeed, he is generally unwilling to seek credit of this type, preferring to finance expansion from windfalls and savings rather than run the risk of foreclosure through default in repayment.

Finally, the informal sector is highly competitive. At one extreme there are established enterprises enjoying a good reputation among a regular clientele; at the other are countless workers employed for only a fraction of the working day and willing to charge the lowest price compatible with their subsistence needs. Whilst such differences exist the latter will aspire to emulate the success of the former; the way appears open to them. The successful artisans intensify competition in training apprentices among whom the market must ultimately be shared. The opportunities for accumulation are meagre indeed and, in addition, the conscious choice to diversify one's activities inhibits the growth of individual enterprises.

In the small provincial town it is possible for artisans and traders to form guilds for the organisation of their respective activities. In the city this becomes well-nigh impossible with the vastly increased numbers involved, say, of tailors or carpenters, and the diversity of their origins.

Even where some formal organisation has been possible the scope of operations is limited. Sanctions which could control competition within the small group become ineffectual in the larger areas; retail traders can evade price-fixing rules. The organisation may contain successful and wealthy operators and poor ones; as Williams (1974) says when he describes the Ibadan beer-sellers, the poor may be dependent upon the wealthy who are in control of the association, and so may be unable to promote their own particular interests. Taxi-drivers may be well organised but in withdrawing their services, in protest against licence fees or police harassment, they provide a public demonstration of their discontent but have little coercive force with which to exact their demands. Domestic servants' associations may draw up ideal conditions of employment but those who strike are too easily dismissed and refused the references essential to continued employment.

Thus organised protest has little effect, either because there are so many other people able and willing to replace the strikers, or because those most disadvantaged by any strike, the consumers, are not those to whom the demands are directed and themselves have little political influence. In either case, the costs to the striker are high; living near or below the poverty line he can ill afford to lose a day's income, let alone his job.

MOVEMENT THROUGH CATEGORIES

In the previous pages we have looked at a variety of modes of urban employment. Some individuals remain within one mode throughout their working life, but one of the characteristic features of Third World cities is the extent to which men and women move between wage employment in the formal sector and informal sector activities.

For the casual labourer, employed in the big firms or public services, the chances of ever attaining a better job are slight. His educational qualifications are probably very low and he learns few new skills in his job. He is likely to pin his hopes on the success of his children (though such children of poor parents are the most disadvantaged in the scholastic race). The permanently employed semi-skilled or skilled worker is little better placed. For a few, perhaps 5 per cent, there are chances of becoming a foreman or supervisor. But again, routine machine-minding creates no new skills. The factory worker, also starting with minimal educational qualifications and physically fatigued by his work and the often long journey to and from it, is far less likely than the clerk or teacher to be studying privately to attain the qualifications which would facilitate his advancement. With wages that are extremely low relative to the subsistence needs of his family and with meagre, if any, formal social security to guard against sickness or unemployment, his chances of accumulating enough earnings to set up his own business are slight. Nevertheless, the hope exists.

For the informal sector artisan or trader, too, the chances of success are slim. He rarely has any social security and though business may produce a sudden windfall the hazards arising from sickness or other misfortunes are great. Life is a game of snakes and ladders. Yet whilst wage employment seems to offer no route to self-advancement, in the informal sector of crafts and trading a route is open; the small retail trader may become a wholesaler, the artisan may take on co-workers and eventually become a trader in the commodity produced, the motor-mechanic may turn to selling spare parts. Trade is usually a more lucrative activity than manufacture.

In these circumstances the wage-earner aspires to enter the informal sector. In West Africa wage employment often implies a subordination which ill befits a man approaching elderhood; he feels like a slave. Such sentiments are not so strongly felt elsewhere; here a simple economic rationality prevails. The informal sector is seen as providing more opportunities for advancement, and as a man becomes older and less able to compete with the young men for jobs requiring strength or stamina, a small business provides security. Again, when so few have retirement pensions but many in their advanced years still have young children to maintain, a continuing income alternative to wage employment is essential.

Yet, although the desire exists, the transition is not easy to make. Saving is difficult, and with the financial responsibilities for one's own family, and perhaps for other kin, increasing with age, the possibility that one can accumulate enough to change jobs quickly without lengthy loss of income is small. Here, though, family involvement may ease the process; the wife can mind the shop during its developing years, the husband taking over on his retirement. A corollary of this process is a wide range in the scale and the profitability of activities within a given sphere; thus Moser (1977) divided the sellers in the Bogota retail market which she studied into three categories: a predominantly young, successful category of sellers, hoping to become wholesalers; a category of elderly traders earning barely enough for their subsistence needs; and a third intermediate category of people who made an adequate living but no more.

We may imagine an idealised urban career pattern. The primary school leaver, whether immigrant or city-born, seeks good wage employment, especially if he is scholastically qualified. But whilst waiting he undertakes a variety of casual jobs, especially in the informal sector. Here he may eventually establish himself. If, however, he obtains wage employment he still aspires to have his own business, whether as a means of advancement or as security for his old age. Thus a man passes from informal to formal and back into the informal sector. The transitions are rarely smooth; King (1977) gives a graphic account of the efforts of a young Kenyan blacksmith to set up his own business. Repeatedly his failures forced him back into wage employment to begin saving anew.

Far more common in practice is the holding of multiple jobs – moonlighting, as it is called in the West. Here the motives are less the long-term aspirations than the current financial needs; a man cannot support his family on his wage. Thus he may work by day in a factory, in the evenings become a taxi-driver and for the remaining hours act as a nightwatchman.

Not only do such strategies have significant repercussions for the household economy, but each form of employment generates its own set of attitudes – collective action and opposition to the bosses in the formal sector, individual achievement and the establishment of a good relationship with patrons and clients in the informal sector.

We have said nothing so far of unemployment and crime, yet official statistics usually record between 10 and 30 per cent of the urban population as unemployed, and the crime rate can be deduced, if not from statistics, at least from the personal insecurity felt by the wealthy (Bairoch, 1973).

Previous paragraphs have, however, indicated the location of unemployment. The school leavers are unemployed as they seek their first jobs; their situation may be ambiguous, for whilst seeking permanent wage employment they undertake a range of jobs, from honest casual employment such as helping a trader or craftsman, to forms which move towards illegality – from 'minding' parked cars, to stealing from them, and all other forms of robbery. Such persons are better described by the West African term 'applicant' – they seek work but are not entirely without it. Many, of course, are 'unemployed' as they move from one job to another, following dismissal, redundancy or the collapse of a firm; or as casual labourers in construction they wait to be hired again. More chronically unemployed are the elderly who cannot sustain regular wage labour, or whose failing powers render them inefficient artisans or traders. Unrecorded are the wives who *would* enter employment, at least in part-time jobs, were the opportunities available to them.

This catalogue demonstrates that the unemployed do not constitute a category with a common set of experiences. All may bemoan the lack of work and attribute their misfortune to faulty government planning, but their aspirations and their strategies vary widely. Each individual sees himself not at the bottom of the social heap but as a marginal member of that stratum which he deems to be his proper location. The unemployed school leaver identifies with the clerks into whose ranks he hopes, with the requisite qualifications, to enter.

A final theme of this chapter, which leads into the substantive issues of the next, is the pattern of personal relationships established in the work situation. Men make friends with their mates on the shop floor, but between casual labourers on a building site relationships are more ephemeral. These men are rarely living side by side in a company compound or barracks; they come from the inner city slums or the shanty towns. Their ties with the neighbours here and, which is more important, with their compatriots in the city, tend to be much stronger. Traders and artisans are even less likely to form close friendships with business peers. Much of the success of workers in the informal sector depends on the maintenance of good personal relationships with suppliers and customers, bureaucrats and clients; these relationships cut across class lines.

We have already seen that a man may hold two or more jobs; and that family members may deliberately choose a variety of occupations. A family may consist of husband, employed in a factory, and his wife, a part-time domestic servant; they collaborate in selling cooked food from an evening stall; their children are successful clerks or traders, and unemployed 'applicants'. The family is an ideological unit; members tend to share values and attitudes in spite of different life and work experiences. The families of the Third World urban poor will reflect this variety.

In city employment the relationships established in the work situation may transcend the primordial ties of ethnicity. Co-workers on the shop floor do not come from a single rural community. Epstein (1958) has described how the copper mine workers of Zambia rejected the attempts of management to work through tribal elders and instead established a trade union to articulate their demands.

Yet in many specific situations work relationships are

reinforced by those of ethnicity (see Sheth, 1968; Holm-ström, 1976; Gupta, 1978, for some Indian examples). Men are expected to recommend their kin for vacancies in their workplace; workers in a Japanese-owned car assembly plant in Peru petitioned that all vacancies should be reserved for kin of established staff. Foremen show preference for compatriots. Men from a certain area may foster the myth that they have a special aptitude for specific tasks – in parts of West Africa some men are viewed as expert well-diggers, though this was not their traditional occupation. (Personnel managers often perpetuate the belief in claiming a monopoly of this esoteric knowledge, and the men concerned are only too happy to retain the monopoly over such tasks.) In a tobacco factory in Zaria, Nigeria, so many of the employees were Tiv that the company trade union and the Tiv ethnic association became virtually coterminous bodies (Remy, 1975). As in national politics, so in union affairs ethnicity can play a significant role in competition for leadership (Lynch, 1969).

In the informal sector, traders in a specific commodity may come from a single village. Diop (1960) reports thus of news-vendors in Dakar, Senegal; Smith (1975) for Lima, Peru, where he studied the people of Huasicancho, a small *sierra* community whose members specialised in hawking fresh fruit in the affluent suburbs of the city. They had no formal means of excluding others but the co-operation which they could extend to each other, and especially to newcomers in advising them how to trade, enabled them to surmount the risks and difficulties which drove others out of business.

In Western industrial societies the great majority of the workforce is in wage employment, and mostly in large enterprises. It is tempting to see a common work situation as creating a uniform consciousness of class. In the Third World we have the overt distinction between formal and informal sectors, the relationship between which in the overall capitalist system is problematic. The two sectors each generate a wide range of relationships between workers leading to trade union activity and patriarchal bonds of varying intensity. Furthermore, having defined some economic categories we find that individuals are passing rather rapidly from one to another, and that several may coexist within family or community. Personal identification with such economic categories is thus weakened, a factor of considerable significance when alternative modes of identification are, as we shall see in the next chapter, relatively pronounced.

4

Social Groupings

In Chapter 2 we noted the distinction between classes defined in terms of man's place in the production process and of his life-style – a distinction between production and consumption. But this distinction must not be seen as a mere economistic one – earning versus spending. In focusing upon production it is often assumed that man's relationships in his workplace subsume all others. The image of the colliery village, in which miners work together at the coalface, live in the same street and drink in the same pub, is a powerful one; social ties here reinforce class solidarity. In the modern city, however, occupational categories do not usually reside together; men enjoy a wide variety of leisure interests. These other social relationships may be significant in the formation of attitudes or the levels of understanding of society.

In describing in the previous chapter the economic categories which predominate in the Third World city, we were using observer's constructs. Of course, a man is conscious of his occupation and its status; but he does not necessarily stress the dichotomy between formal and informal sector activities; he may not appreciate the degree of subordination or exploitation which he experiences; and he may thus be unaware of class interests so defined. In this chapter we focus upon relationships of which the actor is more aware.

We tend in the West to expect that the question 'what are you?' will be answered in occupational terms – a carpenter or a labourer, for instance; that when speaking of 'people like me' a factory worker will be referring to other factory workers. But a social identification in such terms is not necessarily the most salient one. In a vivid description of a Bombay shanty town, Lynch (1974, 1979) has described how one group of men saw themselves as potters, a caste occupation; a second group saw themselves as Adi-Dravidas by origin; whilst a third group saw themselves as Muslims, distinct from the Hindu majority. In the Third World cities ethnic identities such as these can be very powerful (A. Cohen, 1974).

Weber used the term status groups (*Stand*) to refer to such groups. These were for him the basic social divisions in pre-capitalist societies, but they tended to disappear with the development of capitalism for they were antithetical to the emergent classes. (In this sense status groups are very different from Warner's classes.) But the ethnic divisions which are often so marked in Third World cities are not in the process of disappearing – at least not in the immediate future. Although obviously founded on groupings which antedate modern capitalist penetration, the form which they now take is a consequence of contemporary urbanisation. It is, too, the same urbanisation process which determines the form of residential communities which also contribute to social identity.

Social groups defined in ethnic or residential terms may have their own interests, often couched in economic terms and involving power relationships. And just as we can relate classes to each other in a variety of configurations – dichotomous, functional, or in a hierarchical gradation – so too can ethnic or residential groups be ordered. Black may oppose white; a number of ethnic groups or residential communities may be ranked in terms of social prestige. Such groups tend to be far more clearly defined than are social classes; it is far easier for them to enforce closure, in Parkin's terms.

Our task in this chapter is to outline some of the significant features of life in the Third World city, to ascertain the degree to which dominant patterns of social relationships, expressed in ethnic or community terms, either reinforce the economic categories which we have defined or tend to negate them. The observer's constructs are to be contrasted with the experience of the urban poor themselves. We shall look successively at the social networks which people establish in the cities, the forms of ethnic associations which are created and the nature of residential communities.

SOCIAL NETWORKS

Typical among the urban poor are the immigrants from the rural areas. Often they are portrayed as urban peasants, for they retain one foot in the countryside. But the rural link which is so tenaciously maintained is not merely an affective tie; it must be seen in terms of the security which it affords in the urban situation.

For the majority of the urban poor insecurity is their greatest problem (see, for example, Lomnitz, 1977). For those in irregular employment, as building construction labourers or temporary unskilled workers, for instance, there is the continual search for new employment. For those in more stable wage employment, as for all others, fear of illness or such crises is ever present. The artisan or petty trader in the informal sector has little certainty of continuing prosperity. There is in consequence a strong reliance upon those who can provide information about jobs, or introduce one to employers or customers. One's social network is thus a most valued resource; time and energy spent in maintaining it is as important as investing in a savings account – and in conditions of extreme poverty it is much more prevalent. But the network so created is far from congruent with economic, ethnic, or residential categories (Mitchell, 1969; Singh, 1976).

The typical migrant to the city is young; he leaves the rural area between the ages of 15 and 25, perhaps when he finishes primary school. He arrives with very few practical skills appropriate to the urban environment, and little or no financial capital. His emigration is precipitated by the perceived lack of opportunity in the countryside. Farming is stagnant, as governments have done little to change the traditional practices. Land reform measures often involve consolidation of holdings and capital investment, which excludes those with weak tenurial rights. The falling death rate among small children, consequent upon the spread of rural clinics and hospitals, produces in many areas an increased population which cannot be accommodated on the land available. For such as are completely landless permanent emigration seems the only answer. For others, with land, a shorter period of employment in the city is seen as a means of providing an immediate cash input to the household economy – to pay for schooling for younger children, for instance; or as a means of accumulating a little capital – to invest in a piece of land. The young migrant, as yet unmarried, can live frugally.

The first migrants from a backward rural area probably went to a nearby mine or plantation, or to the local provincial towns. Here they met other workers and learned of the bigger towns and cities. They thus eventually reached the metropolis in a series of 'steps'. But once established in this city the process of 'step migration' becomes one of 'chain migration' as later emigrants travel directly to the city, seeing it (quite justifiably in most cases) as the locus of greatest opportunity.

The young migrant arrives, with or without prior warning, and in most cases makes immediately for the house of his closest relatives. Indeed, many will have already spent a holiday there. A smaller number will join their school classmates who have established themselves. The host acknowledges an obligation to provide board and lodging and to help the newcomer to find employment and a permanent place in which to live. Not unnaturally he is anxious to see his lodger independently established as soon as possible and, to this end, he exploits his own network to the full.

The migrant is thus quickly drawn into an established network, consisting most immediately of his close kin in the city, and then other members of the same home area. His reliance upon them in his first weeks in the city creates a reciprocal obligation, so that he in turn must both help those who have helped him and also aid later immigrants.

The migrant does not rupture his relationships with those

in the rural area. His affective ties with his parents and siblings still living there are maintained; they may be sending him presents of foodstuffs, whilst he sends home cash or gifts from the city markets. One important issue is the degree to which the status of the emigrant in the home town or village is maintained throughout his absence. Where the home community is composed of large family groups – lineages or descent groups – in which individual status is determined by age and genealogical position, it is probable that the migrant will be able to return to his natal community and assume whatever privileged position is his due. Conversely a community composed of discrete individual families will not provide this opportunity.

One most important attribute of family membership is, of course, continuing rights in land. Unwelcome though the prospect of a farming career may be, the availability of a plot of land in the village is one of the most important elements in the security of the urban migrant. He may aspire to return in his old age to his village and, in the absence of a pension, maintain himself from his land. Again the home area may offer retirement opportunities in petty trade. Much depends on the degree of development of the home community – whether it offers a potential for small investment, whether it has electricity, water and other amenities enjoyed in the city.

The home village is thus seen, variously, both as the locus of one's ultimate security – a place to retreat to after failure in the city; and of retirement – the place to which one will return in one's old age and where one will finally die. Throughout the Third World this attachment to the home community is stressed, though in varying degrees. It is most strong in African countries with a tribal, or descent group based, social structure (Lloyd, 1967, ch. 8). In Latin America it is strong, for instance, among the Quechua of the Peruvian *sierra*, who again have strongly corporate groups in the village, but weak among the *ladinos* of Guatamala whose home communities are much more individualised (B. Roberts, 1974). For the Indian the status of his caste in his village is probably significant.

Frequently one feels that the aspiration to return to the natal community will never materialise. The children of the city migrants will themselves live and work in the city and it is they who will care for their parents in their old age. The parents will still lack the savings with which to ensure a comfortable rural retirement. But in the meantime the migrant remains oriented towards the members of his home community, both in the city and in the rural area. His relationships with these two sets of people are inter-dependent. For his prestige in the village will, to a high degree, reflect both his individual success in the city and the manner in which he has shared this with his compatriots; a man who has refused to help them when in trouble will find himself ostracised in his village.

The need for security forces the poorer urban migrant into ever-increasing dependence upon his kinsmen, and others from his natal community. He cannot afford to alienate himself from them, for no other social group will admit him and the state itself provides little or no aid. He becomes encapsulated within such an urban community. At the other end of the scale, the better-educated migrant with a secure and relatively well-paid job can free himself from the constraints imposed by such obligations to his kin. He is less concerned with a return to the village; he is less dependent upon his compatriots for security. He can choose, therefore, to seek his friendships outside this narrowly defined group, to participate in a wider variety of urban voluntary associations, membership of which is too costly for the very poor. But he does have a choice, and many have continued to spend most of their leisure time with their compatriots; some, as we shall see later, find it economically advantageous to be active within the ethnic association. For many, it is more satisfying to be a big fish in a little pond than a small fish in the big pond (see Mayer, 1961, for a contrast between two such types of migrant in South Africa).

The social network of compatriots will usually embrace men and women of differing occupations and differently located in the production process. Only in a few cases do such groups monopolise occupational categories; urban caste groups in India are one example, while others have been reported in other contexts – news-vendors in Dakar, fruit-sellers in Lima. Furthermore, the members of the network are variably successful. Migrants from the *sierra* Indian villages of Peru find that their urban advancement is blocked by the entrenched urban *mestizo*; most compatriots are poor, though not equally so. In contrast, in Africa the leading politicians, senior civil servants and successful businessmen have, in very many cases, come from humble villages with which they continue to maintain a close relationship. The present social distance between such men and the urban poor from their own natal communities is, of course, immense. Extreme deference is usually manifest in interaction between persons of the two sets, yet the poor artisan or labourer feels that he has a right to approach his successful compatriot and that the latter has an obligation to help him – an obligation which the latter very often accepts.

Relationships of patronage such as these are not, of course, confined to kinsmen and compatriots. They exist too with employers and many chance acquaintances. Remember here that many of those working in the informal sector are providing goods and services for the affluent rather than the poor. The medical doctor to whom an itinerant trader sells vegetables can be called upon to provide advice on health and employment. Such relationships are cherished, for while the benefits gained may be infrequent and unpredictable when compared with those expected from humble kinsfolk, they may well be of much greater value.

In the Roman Catholic countries of Latin America godparenthood provides a further strong bond between a parent and the co-godparent of his or her child. Such ties may be between social equals, between co-workers for instance; but often the relationship is asymmetrical, strengthening the ties of patronage described above.

ETHNIC ASSOCIATIONS

In the previous section we looked at the ties that exist between kinsmen and members of the natal community at the informal level. Frequently, however, a formal voluntary association (defined in terms of locality, caste, or similar primordial bond) is created to carry out many of the same functions. Officers are selected: very often the first or oldest migrant is chairman, a treasurer collects a monthly subscription and a secretary keeps the minutes of the regularly held meetings. Sometimes these associations are hierarchically ordered; at the lowest level are those of the villages, next come the district associations and above them, perhaps, the provincial bodies. Such has been, for example, the mode of the Ibo associations in Nigeria.

These ethnic associations may be examined in terms of their function, the universality of membership, their ubiquity and their evolution.

Three functions are frequently encountered, although there is no reason why they should always coexist. First, the association is concerned with conditions in the home area. Urban members, having rather more experience of the world, intervene in local politics, perhaps suggesting modes of local development. Money is collected to finance the building of a new road to link the village with the highway, or of a primary school. Such works require the compliance of the government which is expected to maintain the service once it is provided; the level of activity within the association is thus related to the degree to which government is promoting such self-help community development. Again, the better-educated urban members of the association can lobby government officials and agencies to ensure favoured treatment of their own area; even the humble clerk has the opportunity to place the file relating to his own village on top of the pile, and that of a rival community at the bottom.

Secondly, the urban association may formalise the provision of aid to those in distress. Upon the death of a member it may organise the transport of the body and of the immediate family to the home community; money may be donated to those out of work.

Thirdly, the association may present a common front to the outside world. The members may have a quasi-monopoly over a specific economic activity – a particular craft, for instance, or trade in a special commodity; the association acts to preserve these interests. Sometimes, through its material assistance, members can compete more effectively with interlopers and can hope to drive them out of business. In other contexts the association may bargain with government officials to gain licences or preferential treatment. Members are often anxious that their disputes should be settled within the association, that deviance should be controlled by themselves. Police may, in fact, refer cases of fighting between members, or of delinquent or abandoned children, to the leaders of the association.

In some areas one finds that all members of a natal community are at least nominal members of the urban association, and that most are active. Ibo associations tend to be of this kind and a typical one may include both senior civil servants or university lecturers and the unskilled poor. On the other hand the membership of the association may be restricted to the poor, as Jeffries (1978) reports for Takoradi in Ghana. In the latter case the emphasis of the association's activities tends to be on the social security of its poorer members; the more successful and wealthy tend to drop out in order to evade their obligations. But these obligations may not always be easily denied; an Ibo, for instance, who refused to participate in the activities of his own association would probably find himself ostracised not only in his own natal community but also by Ibos of other communities who felt that his behaviour fell short of that expected by members of this ethnic group. Small business-men may feel that the demands in time and money made by their association are inimical to the development of their trade. Others, however, may be heavily reliant on the support of urban and rural members for the success of their enterprises; a leadership role in the association is here an adjunct to business activity.

Ethnic associations are not equally well developed throughout the Third World. Thus in general it is the ethnic groups with a tribal social structure that have the strongest associations. In the cities of Africa they are numerous, although not all ethnic groups are similarly represented. Migrants who are in a very subordinate position and fear discrimination against themselves are more likely to organise than are members of the dominant ethnic group. An ethnic identity may be as much imposed on these minorities by the dominant groups as created by themselves (Basch, 1978).

As members of a rural community prosper in the town and as their home village also develops, so we should expect the nature of the association to change. Transformations of this kind have been described in Peru (Skeldon, 1976, 1977; Altamirano, 1980). The association of the remote backward village enjoys the support of all urban members of the community; its activities are focused upon village improvement and urban social security. But wealthier rural areas with a large number of migrants in Lima, many of whom are quite prosperous, tend to have a proliferation of associations, some being oriented towards self-help among the poor, others towards enhancing the business interests of the richer members and becoming lobbies for specific demands. In Lima, in fact, the provincial clubs are of a very different character from the village associations; they are dining clubs of the successful urban elite, equivalent in their function to the masonic lodges or rotary clubs of the UK (Jongkind, 1974).

In the preceding pages we have explored the emergence of ethnic identity through the development of personal networks and the creation of ethnic associations of compatriots. The emphasis has been on small local groups. However, strong ethnic consciousness transcends these relationships – they are only some of the possible manifestations of it (see, for example, Nair, 1978). Marxists assume that a level of class-consciousness exists in which all spheres of activity are subsumed within production relationships; such a level is difficult to find in the real world – but ethnic consciousness can approach this level more closely. Ethnic loyalty tends to be a more powerful sentiment than class interest.

Evocation of ethnic identity exists in different situations. In one, the 'ethnics' are minorities, perhaps recent immigrants (as are Pakistanis and West Indians in Britain, Turks, Portuguese, Algerians in France and Germany), contrasted with a culturally homogeneous dominant population. Here ethnicity reinforces the experience of subordination. In a contrasting situation, common in Africa, rich and poor all come from the same range of ethnic groups. Competition for high office is seen in ethnic terms, as is competition for the lowliest employment; the former serves to maintain the dominance of 'tribalism' as a social process. Rivalry between ethnic groups overrides the class struggle. In a third situation ethnicity becomes transposed as nationalism – all citizens share a common ethnic heritage and are opposed to those of other countries. Lubeck (1978, 1979), in describing the development of worker-consciousness in Kano, Nigeria, has graphically described how class awareness is both obscured and enhanced by the belief that Islam is a minority religion. In the 1960s radical leaders of some newly independent African states argued that classes did not exist within their societies; the struggle lay between their states and the erstwhile metropolitan powers.

RESIDENTIAL ASSOCIATIONS

Members of an ethnic community may be settled in a relatively few residential areas within the city; early migrants tend to find accommodation for latecomers near to their homes. But it is rare for all members of the ethnic community to live exclusively in a single area – they tend, in fact, to be dispersed throughout the city. Residential communities are therefore ethnically heterogeneous (Peattie, 1968; Wiebe, 1975; Lomnitz, 1977).

Between neighbours the same types of relationship may develop as between members of an ethnic group. They may provide mutual aid to each other; they may collectively organise for the defence or improvement of the neighbourhood. As we shall see, community associations are not highly developed in all residential areas (see, for example, B. Roberts, 1973), but it may well be that membership of such an association is the only form of organised activity open to the artisan or petty trader who does not belong to a trade union and who has no ethnic association.

As the industrial towns of nineteenth-century Europe grew, housing was provided for the migrants by public and private developers. Streets of uniform houses were built, each attracting residents within a relatively narrow income range and enjoying in consequence a similar style of life. In the Third World city most of the new housing of the poor has been constructed by the migrants themselves, and one consequence is the great heterogeneity of design and quality. Neighbourhoods are thus more like those of the medieval city, in which rich and poor are closely juxtaposed.

Most Third World cities have their inner city slums comprising both the decaying homes of the affluent who have moved out to the expensive suburbs and purpose-built tenements. Governments, however, are too poor to provide cheap housing on a large scale – or they prefer to allocate their resources elsewhere. Such low-cost housing projects as have been completed are usually constructed to high Western standards of design and finish so that only middle-range executives can afford them. Private construction companies prefer to build for the relatively wealthy who can make substantial down payments and provide good security for a mortgage to be repaid in a comparatively short time. Little or nothing is done for the poor. For the newly arrived migrant residence in the inner city is often advantageous, for it is here that casual employment will probably be found. But rents tend to be high and, with the increasing flow of emigrants from the rural areas, the housing situation becomes acute. Two contrasting situations may be illustrated here.

The land of the periphery of Lagos is still held under

customary forms of tenure by the indigenous descent groups. Their elders have sold off single house plots to whoever can afford to buy and to build a house. Some sales are to the relatively poor who build a small mud-walled house with a corrugated iron roof; building regulations are here minimal. Other sales are to the more successful, who build a two-storey house, using superior materials. Frequently the owner lives on the top floor, renting the ground floor to one or more poorer families. Though differences in wealth separate the landlord from his tenants, both may share a similar cultural heritage and similar experiences in migrating to the city. Other purchasers build houses specifically for renting, and here too a number of families may occupy a single building, sharing communal cooking and toilet facilities.

In other cities of Africa, as in most Latin American cities, the peripheral land is held either as private estates of the rich or as public domain. The poor cannot obtain individual plots on which to build. They have therefore invaded land illegally, and often in spectacular fashion. Close friends and associates secretly plan for many months; one night an invasion by hundreds of families is organised, and temporary structures are erected to give squatters' rights. The property-owners and police counter these moves with some show of force but in most cases the authorities acquiesce in the invasion for this is in fact the simplest solution to the housing problem. Over the years the invaders build their own houses. Such settlements tend to be predominantly of owner-occupiers, although in time subletting and small-scale landlordism can develop (Mangin, 1967; Dietz, 1980; Lloyd, 1980).

The mode of urban development in each of these cases leads to social heterogeneity in the neighbourhood. In the first case land was sold indiscriminately to rich and poor buyers so that superior- and inferior-quality houses are juxtaposed. In the better houses tenants may be accommodated, their rents enabling the owner to further his building activities. So the rich merchant lives close by the poor labourer; the skilled artisan still 'lives over the shop'.

In the second case one finds that the invaders, all previously resident in the city, have different resources. Some are in secure employment, others are only casually employed; some have education and savings, others have not. Some therefore quickly build a decent house while others continue to live in shacks built of waste materials. But for a variety of reasons the former cannot move to a better suburb; their house is of idiosyncratic design and construction and has little market value; its sale would enable them to move only into a smaller house on a residential estate – and their family is growing; often in such estates homes may not be used for business purposes – one cannot use the front room as a shop or workplace. Similarly, the very poor have no incentive to move; they pay no rent for house or land, and no rates; they would not be more cheaply accommodated elsewhere.

Thus the more affluent among the urban poor and the very poor live side by side; they are not segregated into stratified residential zones (MacEwen, 1974). Ties of mutual aid, of patronage, of godparenthood, develop among them. Intermarriage is facilitated. But one may find, too, more intense feelings of envy and disapprobation. The poor are jealous of the success of the rich; the latter are concerned, as we shall see in the next chapter, about their own achievement and see the failure of their neighbours in terms familiar to middle classes everywhere – of laziness, weak moral fibre, and the like.

Little community organisation is found in the inner city slums. The landlord–tenant relationship is an individual one; tenants are perhaps transient and aspiring to move out of the shanty towns. In Lagos the suburbs described above form part of a local government structure which the local elite of big traders and educated professionals tends to dominate. It is in the shanty town that one tends to find strong community associations. First, the invasion and subsequent defence of the settlement is highly organised and necessitates the active participation of most members. Secondly, these areas are usually seen as external to the city's municipal government – the people pay no rates and thus receive no services as a right. They may, however, be encouraged to acquire basic services through their provision of free labour and payment for materials. In many cities this has been quite an effective mode of development. Implicit in this mode, however, is the dependence upon government which is fostered – the community leaders must beg and cajole, but not oppose, the city bureaucrats. Again, local communities are competing with each other; government has limited resources and if one area gets water or electricity, another is having to go without. Some Peruvian ideologues have extolled this competitive self-help as inhibiting the development of a class-consciousness deriving from the common experience of poverty. Yet, liberal though government policies of self-help and community development appear at one level, they do tend to maintain the stark distinction between the urban poor in their shanty towns and the rich in their affluent suburbs. The belief that the former can substantially improve their condition is, furthermore, probably ill-founded. Whilst such shanty town settlements can organise their own defence and obtain minimal services, the disparities of wealth which later develop create such divergent interests that collective action is inhibited (see Pickvance, 1976; Castells, 1977).

CONCLUSION

Much of what has been described in the previous pages is pertinent also to cities of the industrial West, but Third World cities differ from these both qualitatively and quantitatively. Except among the immigrant populations one does not, in the West, find such a high degree of ethnicity. Urban development tends not to produce active residential associations. Nor do ethnicity and shanty towns and their correlates seem to be disappearing in the Third World in the supposed modernisation process. In fact they are a direct consequence of the particular mode of development which is taking place.

Much of the wage employment in the cities is of a casual

nature, employment is for short periods, and a very high proportion of the working population is engaged in very small enterprises or in self-employment in the informal sector. To the insecurity occasioned by the uncertainties of income is added insecurity about sickness and death – against which no protection exists in state social security. Protection is, however, gained from kin and compatriots both in the urban area and in the natal community from which the townsman has emigrated. Furthermore state provision of cheap housing and urban services is minimal; the migrant attempts to fulfil his basic needs by his own individual effort and through residential associations.

Organised activity based upon occupation, ethnicity and residence is far from evenly distributed. A man may belong to a trade union but not to ethnic or residential associations; or an ethnic or residential association could well be the only organisation to which he belongs. In some respects these three modes of association may be complementary. There is no reason why a man cannot be an active member in each of them. In practice, however, there may be over-lapping of function – if help in time of sickness is provided by compatriots, workers will not expect their trade union to offer this service, and their involvement in the union will be less. Time, money and leadership are scarce resources and those expended in one form of association will not be available to others.

In both ethnic and residential associations one finds that the members span a wide range of occupations and income; they embrace the very poor and the relatively affluent, the clerk or skilled factory worker in regular employment and the casual labourer or self-employed artisan. The occupational categories set out in the previous chapter do not provide the basis for perceived social divisions.

Unfortunately little research has been carried out into the terms used by the urban poor to describe themselves. A common pattern, perhaps, is that where one term describes the 'common man', who manages to subsist and who upholds the dominant norms of his society; ranked beneath him are those who fall below this subsistence level and are forced into 'anti-social' behaviour; above are the slightly better off. The Yoruba terms *mekunnu, talaka* and *olowo* exemplify this pattern (Lloyd, 1974, pp. 168–9; Gutkind, 1975).

A further attribute of ethnic and residential associations is the competition which they engender among the urban poor. Men help their own kin in the competition for jobs; traders try to reserve for their compatriots a quasi-monopoly in certain commodities; residential communities compete to win a share of the meagre government aid to gain piped water or a new school. In the West local radical politicians have in the past strongly opposed all such associational activity as inhibiting the development of a united working-class consciousness. Latterly, however, such leaders have sought to work through these associations, hoping both to ameliorate the conditions of the poor and to educate them about the cause of their poverty (Cowley *et al.*, 1977). In the Third World city this element of radical education tends to be absent; instead one finds the ideology of self-help being extolled at all levels. For government it provides a liberation of local resources, enabling it to divert its own funds elsewhere; for the liberal of the dominant classes it gives dignity to the poor, eroding the apathy that stems from paternalism. The poor are encouraged to supplicate for the aid which they need, rather than demand it and oppose their government.

The obvious differences in wealth among the urban poor and the relationships produced by their work situation are thus cross-cut by ties of ethnicity and residence, each of which may provide the basis for a strong sense of identity; associations of both type socialise the city-dweller from an early age. A marked stratification of the urban poor is thus prevented. However, these associations may serve to intensify the experience of deprivation. Thus the shanty town resident is aware of the marked disparity between his neighbourhood and the nearby affluent suburbs. Members of an ethnic group may feel that they are discriminated against in their struggle for advancement. But in other situations all ethnic groups may be competing equally, and each may have its representatives in the upper strata. Thus a poor artisan may complain that 'those in power' do nothing for men such as himself, yet he will approach a compatriot who is in just such a dominant position for help. The opposition between rich and poor is muted by relationships of patronage, both within and outside the ethnic sphere.

5

Political Action

Class action is frequently discussed only in terms of industrial strikes or of specific forms of political protest – voting patterns and membership of radical political parties, for instance. In this book, however, our task is to explore the various dimensions of class and we must therefore pose a much more general question: how do people react to inequality? What is the response of the urban poor of the Third World cities to the glaring differences in wealth and power which they perceive? (Zeitlin, 1967; Wolpe, 1970; Cornelius, 1970, 1975; Ross, 1973; Gutkind, 1973, 1975; Sandbrook and Cohen, 1975; Eckstein, 1977; Sandbrook and Arn, 1977; Booth and Seligson, 1978; Seligson and Booth, 1979; Nelson, 1979).

Their responses may take two forms: they may accept the existing social system, the pattern of relationships which determines the allocation of wealth and power, and try to maintain or improve their position within it; alternatively, they may seek to change the system, altering the rules which govern the opportunities open to them and their chances of exploiting them.

Again, their efforts may be individually oriented, each person seeking his own gain, presumably at the expense of others. Or collectively men may combine to seek a common goal. Most individual action is set within the context of the existing system; single-handed one cannot hope to change it. Collectively one may change it; but nevertheless much collective action is competitive as groups vie with each other to maintain or advance their social position.

Each mode of action presupposes a model of the actor's

perception of society, this model being, however, a construct of ourselves as observers. The actor may be seen to use a variety of models, each being appropriate to specific situations. But we cannot close our discussion with descriptions of actions which are consequent upon models, for actions have unintended consequences; actors may misjudge the situation through incompetence, lack of information and the like; the cumulative effect of their actions may have been difficult, if not impossible, to predict. Events which observers interpret as evidence of class struggle may seem unrelated to the attitudes and motives of individual actors.

In this chapter we shall look, in turn, at the patterns of social mobility in the Third World cities and the aspirations frequently met there; at the emergence of populist modes of government in which political bodies seek mass support yet do little to benefit the poor; and at the failure of groups located outside the urban poor, radical political parties, for instance, to mobilise them.

SOCIAL MOBILITY AND ACHIEVEMENT

In the past two decades a new image of the urban poor has been created. They are dynamic and achievement-oriented, and they live in 'slums of hope' rather than in 'slums of despair'. The latter term characterises the inner city slums and their downwardly mobile residents who are the dropouts of society, the former peripheral shanty towns peopled largely by immigrants. This new image of the shanty town residents contrasts markedly with that given in the 'culture of poverty' literature in which the poor are apathetic, disorganised and aggressive (Lewis, 1967, but see too Leacock, 1971); it contrasts too with a Western stereotype of the working-class man as accepting his subordinate position in society, neither seeing the possibility of, nor aspiring to, rise out of his class.

This new image of the Third World urban poor is undoubtedly founded upon reality. It derives, for the most part, from those who have lived or worked closely with the poor. It is espoused by liberals who seek to restore dignity to the poor and by governments which see in the perceived potential for self-help an excuse for allocating little from the state budget – let the poor raise themselves by their own boot straps. But the pendulum has now swung too far in this direction. The image of the striving 'petit bourgeois' obscures the tensions which do exist. The virtues of striving to get ahead can also be interpreted as an unending struggle to stay afloat. And people *are* happy most of the time because depression is the first stage in failing to cope.

The emphasis on achievement reflects the past experiences of the urban poor and the economic situation in which they are now placed.

In migrating to the city and establishing themselves there, they have succeeded. Surveys frequently report that the migrants have not fulfilled their wildest dreams, but most are happy with their move. It is difficult to express the move in terms of social mobility; is a job as an unskilled labourer in the city better than being a poor farmer? One can with difficulty calculate real income in each category, accounting for services provided by family and friends, for foodstuffs domestically produced or collected. Most migrants see their city homes as an improvement upon their rural ones; frequently they have water nearby, and electricity; clinics and schools are not too distant. Most important, however, is their perception of the opportunities available in the city. In the stagnating rural areas they saw no future for themselves other than that experienced by their fathers; in the city they can launch their families into the modern world. The migrating parents have established a foothold on this launching pad; it is their children, they hope, who will shoot forwards.

The city economy into which the migrant is drawn is one of great recent expansion; new opportunities are continually being created as public services are extended, as new factories open and as new markets are opened up by the rapidly growing population in all income strata. Furthermore, there is considerable diversity in the economic structure with the coexistence of formal and informal sectors.

The migrant thus sees his future not in terms of a succession of similar wage-earning factory jobs but of exploiting an ever-changing pattern of opportunities – of finding his way through a maze to the ultimate rewards of success.

A good wage-earning job may be a stage along this route but it is not, save for the highly skilled, an end in itself. For most men and women such employment is semi- or un-skilled. The possibility of advancement is very limited, for the higher positions demand educational levels beyond that already attained by the poor. And while teachers and clerks can continue studying for higher qualifications, the energy and time expended by the manual labourer in his work inhibits further study. In the Third World a marked cleavage still exists between the manual worker who can expect little change in his status during his lifetime and the white-collar worker who, even in the humblest job, sees himself on the rungs of a career ladder.

However, as we have seen in Chapter 3, the informal sector does seem to offer opportunities for advancement. Incomes of the average artisan or trader may well be commensurate with those of labourers on the minimum wage, but the possibility of success in developing a small enterprise is apparent. Wage-earning is evaluated as a means of acquiring skills and savings with which to establish one's own business. The aspiration of being one's own master does not only accord with the supposed 'peasant mentality' which the migrant brings to the city – a preference for doing things in his own time, and in his own way; it is also a perfectly rational approach to the labour market (Portes, 1972).

But, as many have pointed out, aspirations do not necessarily accord with reality. The chances of accumulating enough savings to start a viable business are slim. The competition between enterprises in the informal sector is severe and the increasing number of new entrants merely depresses the income of them all, making success even more remote. Yet such statistical realities are overridden by the visibility of the few that have been outstandingly successful and who serve as an inspiration to others to follow along the same path. Thus while observer-economists may describe the proletarianisation of the informal sector workers, these workers themselves see their life in terms of the continual struggle to exploit new opportunities. They are as concerned to get ahead as is the white-collar worker on his career ladder; the means of achieving success, however, are different.

Most parents among the immigrant poor are content with securing stable employment in the city; their meagre resources, in education as in savings, do not encourage them to aspire, realistically rather than in fantasy, to any great advancement. But they do entertain such hopes for their children, through their education. The superiority of city schools and in particular the availability of secondary and post-secondary education was, for many, one motive for migration.

Education liberates. With reading one can comprehend the world; specifically one can understand the written rules which constrain one's activities. Parents still, in the absence of retirement pensions, look to their children to care for them in their old age, and the better educated one's children, the brighter one's hopes. Education is necessary for urban employment; for the most menial of tasks one usually has to produce a primary school certificate. Where, as in post-colonial Africa, the output of secondary schools and universities has barely kept pace with the creation of salaried posts, the attainment of a good qualification has guaranteed the appropriate income. Low status in traditional society, in coming from a slave family or from a remote subordinate village in the kingdom, can be negated through education; such an incentive has resulted in many educated people rising from such social strata. However, where the number with qualifications greatly exceeds the jobs available, as in India, for a notorious example, or Latin America, social status resumes its importance; one needs to have the right connections to get the good jobs.

The urban poor are thus highly concerned to further their children's education. In their shanty towns one of their first collective efforts is, very often, to build a school. One never hears a father say 'the education that was good enough for me, is good enough for my son'; all want their sons to be better educated. But whilst an educated parent can help a child with lessons, the barely literate can only ensure that their children attend school regularly, and fulfil the demands made; they are reluctant to discuss their children's progress with the teachers. With such handicaps, together with the fact that the schools attended by the urban poor are usually the worst in the system, the chances that the children will be able to compete successfully with those from the more affluent strata are remote. Yet a route to higher education does exist for them, and here too there are visible examples of those who have traversed it. Efforts to get one's children through the system exceed those made to criticise or remedy it.

Balancing the aspirations are the frustrations; very few do in fact succeed. But the explanation of failure lies to a large extent in personal terms. One lacked the requisite resources; one was cheated; one was unlucky in not obtaining the contract that went instead to a neighbour. The response is to try again – or to give up, to return to the rural areas; and although the migrant is often reluctant to reappear at home, a confessed failure, this escape route does exist. If it is simply bad luck that explains a lack of success, one can but wait and hope that something will turn up eventually.

Such explanations are not incompatible with the ideas of those who see failure in terms of the structure of society, but they do compete with them. Poverty can be explained by low wages in the capitalist system; this system has its impact on the paucity of social services available to the poor; social barriers may deny the poor access to better positions. But such explanations require a deeper understanding of the social system. And when a man compares his own failure with the success of his neighbour, the explanation must be in personal terms, for both are assumed to operate within the same structural constraints.

The actor who looks at the world in the manner discussed in the previous paragraphs uses an egocentric model. He is at the centre of his universe surrounded successively by family and kin, neighbours and peers, and more casual acquaintances. It is his personal network which is the dominant feature of the model – relationships which are seen, in part, in terms of debts and credits, of resources to be manipulated. Central in the model are people like himself; on the fringes are others who are different. An 'us'/ 'them' dichotomy here develops. The category 'us' may be almost coterminous with the urban poor. The limits will be more clearly defined in a stratified society, as in Andean states of Latin America where the rural Indian or the *mestizo* is contrasted with the white oligarchy; they are less clearly defined in Africa, for example, where members of the natal rural community may be in the highest social positions. It is within this 'us' category that social mobility is seen to be possible. People may be ranked hierarchically in terms of income but such distinctions are overridden by those of origin, kinship and neighbourhood. As in Western industrial countries with high rates of immigration, almost everyone is upwardly mobile to some extent as successive new migrants enter at the bottom of the social ladder.

Such a model serves to stress the homogeneity of the urban poor; but it also serves to create a dichotomous model of society. The emphasis placed on achievement and mobility is on social movement within the broadly defined class and not across its boundaries into the class of 'them'. But again, whilst this egocentric model is not incompatible with the dichotomous model, perhaps stressing conflict, its salience in the minds of the poor could result in their expenditure of more effort in attempting to improve their status within the existing structure of society, and less in trying to change society.

COLLECTIVE ACTION

In the previous chapter we saw how two forms of relationship, that based on natal village or town and that based on the urban residential community, provide the basis for collective action. For the many who belong to no trade union (or whose membership is ineffectual) such collectivities provide the sole basis for organised action. I emphasised the degree to which these associations produced competition among the urban poor; one sought to get a new school or road for the home village, rather than have these services allocated to another settlement; one strove to get water and electricity to one's own shanty town, knowing well that another community would have to wait. The rules of the game, as perceived, are that one mobilises one's resources and one begs favours of government officials. To argue that government ought to be providing far more services for distribution is altogether a different game with other rules; it is a dangerous game, too, for one stands to lose not only the increased services sought but also one's own share of the minimal allocation. The attitudes generated by such activity are highly congruent with those pertinent to the individual striving for advancement. Self-help is emphasised. The cause of failure is seen to lie in the inability of a community to mobilise its resources, through lack of mutual trust, indolence, or apathy.

As many have stressed, the fundamental problem of the villages and shanty towns is not their lack of services but their poverty; low incomes precede an inability to pay for services. One must look, therefore, to collective attempts to raise incomes. In Chapter 3 we saw that well-organised trade unions existed in the larger, often foreign-controlled, private firms; in smaller, indigenously owned enterprises a repressively paternalistic management has tended to crush such collective activity. Many of the public services – railways, for example – were highly organised, but seasonally employed labour in both public and private enterprises owed little allegiance to a union.

For many writers the occurrence of strikes is a sufficient evidence of class-consciousness; little is done to examine the level of consciousness thus demonstrated. Other writers have more recently studied the strike process at the micro-level and have given us insight into the workers' understanding of their situation and their actions which followed from this. They have subsequently traced the repercussions of these events. From such studies it can be seen that a relatively low level of class-consciousness among workers may ultimately lead, through a dramatic series of strikes, to a radical or even revolutionary change in a country's government. But to argue thus is very different from positing an abstract high level of consciousness, of which the workers themselves are unaware, as the determinant of subsequent events.

The capitalist enterprise necessarily creates a situation of conflict. To raise profits the management must curtail wages and get more work from the employees. The workers, for their part, resist such attempts. It is usually quite clear to them, and especially so in the smaller enterprise, that their product is being sold for much more than the cost of their labour and that the wealth of the owners/managers accounts for part of the difference. Their natural inclination to protest may be curbed variously by a belief that managers should be highly rewarded for their skills, by paternalism and by repression. But from the earliest periods of capitalist development workers have protested, expressing themselves in the bargaining process, through go-slows or verbal abuse of management, and ultimately through strikes.

There must be two parties to a strike, workers and management, for such an event denotes the breakdown (or absence) of conciliation and bargaining procedures. Workers' militancy faces management's intransigence; but the terms militancy and intransigence cover a variety of concepts.

Workers are described as militant if their demands are quantitatively large – if they demand a 100 per cent rather than a 10 per cent wage increase. They are militant, too, if their demands are presented in a sophisticated manner, suggesting a high level of class-consciousness. But workers are often described as militant when their actions are noisy and violent, in situations when perhaps their demands are minimal or demonstrate very little class-consciousness but when they feel that they have been cheated by non-fulfilment of promises, or that they are unable to communicate with the management. In a like manner the intransigent attitude of management may be related to economic factors – the peculiar situation of their firm or the general state of the national economy makes it difficult for them to meet demands; or their intransigence may be related to factors of personality, the hawks seeking a show-down with workers, the doves urging conciliation. Both sides weigh the effect of sanctions used against them, such as the withdrawal of labour, or dismissal from employment.

Strikes typically revolve around two issues: wage demands and worker discipline. In each case demands may be couched in a variety of ways. Class-conscious workers would be expected to relate wages to their firm's profits, demanding a greater share of the cake. But much more typical of Third World countries is the relating of wage levels to inflation. A minimum wage is set by government in accord with an assumed poverty datum line and firms are expected to conform. Arguments about the amount of the minimum wage are distanced from any discussion of productive relationships. Disputes about worker discipline rarely involve the issues of worker control and production. Unfair dismissals are often seen in ethnic terms: a man is sacked by the foreman through ethnic antipathy or a failure in communication between the two men.

Against what or whom are the workers striking – against capitalist relations of production or a management seen in highly personal terms? More often it is the latter and this is demonstrated by the frequency of personal violence against individual members of management; they are locked in their offices, or their cars are upturned. Company-based unions reinforce this tendency to set demands within the context of the individual firm. However, opposition to the management in multinational companies may be deflected into nationalistic themes by the indigenous government and its agents, who imply that the evils are inherent in foreign domination, not in capitalism; indigenous businesses thus escape opprobrium.

The very visibility of strikes results in their becoming a focal issue in any discussion of class formation; too often it is forgotten that a relatively small proportion of the urban poor are so effectively organised. But one theme in the labour aristocracy thesis asserts that there is a marked cleavage within the urban poor between the established and well-paid workers in the big companies and those in irregular employment or in the informal sector. The former, it is alleged, are able through their trade union activities to attain privileges, such as a high income and security, denied to the unorganised masses. Furthermore, these privileges are gained at the expense of the masses who thus feel both envious and exploited. A critical examination of this thesis is reserved for the concluding chapter of this book; here it is pertinent to state that empirical studies seem to deny the cleavage. The privileges of good wage employment are, furthermore, widely sought and one does not seek to diminish the perquisites of a job to which one aspires, either for oneself or for one's children.

Although the empirical studies tend to portray trade union activity as highly economistic, workers have little consciousness of the workings of a capitalist mode of production and almost no vision of an alternative structure of society to which their actions and struggles might lead. This of course is quite understandable.

The urban workers have received very little education and their experiences of wage employment are limited. Many aspire, not to continued and improved wage employment, but either to a return to the rural area or to self-employment in the city. In a few cases workers in a single enterprise co-reside in a company compound, railway workers in Kampala (Grillo, 1973, 1974) and tin miners in Bolivia (Nash, 1979), for example, and their class-consciousness seems relatively developed; most workers in the modern factories live dispersed through many suburbs.

Trade unions do not provide a radical leadership. Often they have been developed by government initiative and are designed to operate in an economistic manner. Independent states have endeavoured either to co-opt the trade union movement or to repress it; in Ghana, for instance, the movement constituted a wing of Nkrumah's Convention

People's Party. Repression may take the form of restrictive legislation – military governments in Nigeria outlawed strikes (admittedly ineffectually); or of arbitrary violence – in Latin American states prominent trade unionists get arrested or murdered. The impact of trade union activity is lessened by the cleavage between leaders and the rank-and-file members; the latter see the former as corrupt and career-seeking, little attuned to the demands of the workers and more likely to try to make political capital out of a locally initiated strike than to organise workers into collective activity.

Finally, as we shall see in a later section of the chapter, little radical leadership has come from opposition political parties.

Some writers suggest that each successive strike adds to the cumulative experience of the working class and increases its revolutionary potential. This argument reifies the class; the experience of individual workers who spend only a few years in wage employment is much less significant, although, as Grillo (1973, 1974) has shown, workers may well be proud of the past militancy of their colleagues. It could be more convincingly argued that the low level of class-consciousness manifested in these protests suggests that they can continue indefinitely without altering the economic structure of society.

Whilst strikes are instigated as rather parochial movements with limited aims, they may well escalate beyond the intentions or comprehension of their leaders. As we shall see below, the focal issue may become the level of the minimum wage, and government becomes a prime actor rather than an arbiter between management and workers. Opposition to the government is couched in most general terms and wins wide support not only among the wage employees but also among the self-employed; markets may close, or taxis leave the streets.

Even strikes restricted to specific sectors can be very damaging to government and its allies – public sector strikes in railways or electricity, strikes in factories or mines, variously halt the process of administration, the export-oriented economy, or the provision of consumer goods for the affluent strata. Governments are fragile and easily toppled by rival political parties or by military coups when they appear unable to cope with the situation. But the conditions outlined above make it unlikely that the workers will be sufficiently well organised to play a significant role in subsequent events. The incoming government either repressively enforces the *status quo ante* or initiates such limited reforms as will defuse tension without radically affecting the structure of society.

POPULISM

Three themes constantly recur in descriptions of the political activity of the urban poor. Two have already been discussed. First, there is the achievement orientation of the urban immigrants who perceive an upward mobility, an improvement in their lives, in establishing themselves at least for their children. The second is the economism of most local trade union activity and the absence of a radical ideology in the higher echelons of the movement, contributing to a failure to perceive clearly any alternative form of industrial society. Nevertheless, equally widely reported is a dichotomous view of society in which the underprivileged are seen as oppressed by the dominant groups. But 'them' in the context are not the capitalists, the owners of the means of production, but the government.

It is understandable that the poor should conceptualise the opposed group in this way. The owners of the large, probably foreign and multinationally owned, firms are invisible to the workers; the latter can have little appreciation of the complexities of international finance. The owners of the usually very small indigenous firms are viewed paternalistically. Thus neither group provides a clear focus for discontent. The government is in fact a major employer of labour – in many countries employing half the workforce. It is responsible not only for the bureaucratic apparatus of government but also for most services, railways, electricity undertakings, and the like, and perhaps for much industrial production too. Governments thus set the pattern of wages through their own practices. They further control wage levels through the fixing of a minimum wage supposed to reflect a poverty level below which no worker should fall. The larger companies often pay in excess of the minimum wage, but one finds frequently that higher wages are expressed in terms of multiples of the minimum wage; thus a skilled craftsman might earn twice or three times the minimum wage. Small firms and individual employers, on the other hand, may pay below the minimum wage, their employees facing dismissal (if they protest) with little prospect of alternative employment except of a commensurate underpaid nature. Government's wage legislation is thus a focus of organised action, and is of direct concern to all workers.

Government regulations have, too, a direct impact on levels of consumption. Prices of staple commodities may be fixed; marketing boards may purchase foodstuffs directly from the peasant farmers and sell them in the urban areas at subsidised prices. In this way an important element in the demand for a higher minimum wage is negated. It is usually within the power of governments to control rents, though these powers are little used. Government permits, or represses, the establishment of squatter settlements; it endeavours, or fails, to provide low-cost housing.

Government also controls the development of small enterprises in the informal sector. Street trading may be permitted in some areas, banned in others; traders and artisans may need licences to carry on their business. Government may, though it rarely does, establish credit facilities for small businessmen.

In general the governments of Third World states claim to control the economy. At regular intervals a development plan is produced outlining the projected path of progress. The success of such plans and the ultimate well-being of the people is thus directly attributed to the government.

But who are the government and how do they exploit or oppress the poor – if, indeed, they do so?

The wealth of those associated with government contrasts

starkly with the lack of wealth of the urban poor. 'The government lives on the backs of the poor' is a frequent assertion. It seems fairly clear to most that the high salaries of the rich are paid for by the poor. But direct forms of exploitation are not always easy to discover. A clear case of exploitation is seen in the retention by a marketing board of a substantial part of the ultimate selling price of a peasant's crop, the board's surplus then being used to 'finance development'. Most government employees, however, are providing services, not producing goods. It is easier to understand that poverty is the result of low productivity. The primitive subsistence farmer is poor because he grows so little, not because he is exploited by others. His present subordination determines the degree to which the state might help him to produce more. This idiom may be carried over into the urban sphere. The tailor who makes only ten shirts in a week is scarcely exploited; he is restrained from making more. In this situation it is reasonable to believe that certain people are rich because they work harder; the high salary of the educated man is a legitimate reflection of his present skills and the years of effort spent in acquiring them.

The modes by which a modern government controls the economy are so complex that one can scarcely expect the urban poor to understand the process. Even if certain ministries are seen to be involved in certain legislation, government corporately holds responsibility. Presidents and prime ministers are at the apex of the government but this term extends to embrace both elected politicians and senior civil servants and those engaged in parastatal enterprises. It embraces, too, both private professionals and public servants involved in maintaining the system. It is indeed a euphemism for the ruling/dominant class/elite in sociological jargon.

Occupational factions within the category are only dimly perceived. The absence of a large number of wealthy indigenous businessmen inhibits the creation of a distinction between capitalists and officials. The 'government' also displays marked social homogeneity. In Latin American countries it still largely represents the white oligarchy. In Africa its members, although often from humble and ethnically diverse homes, have had similar educational experiences. Intermarriage is common; members live together in the affluent suburbs, belonging to a small number of exclusive clubs.

The mass of the urban poor see two ways in which to articulate their demands. Individually, they may approach their patrons for favours or services on behalf of themselves or their community. Collectively, their activities may culminate in mass protest – employees strike and the self-employed withdraw their services. Such outbursts may develop from small beginnings in one or two factories, but with their escalation the nature of the demands becomes much more generalised, into an accusation of government inactivity or intransigence. Twice in a single decade, in 1964 and 1972, Nigeria experienced such a wave of protest, when the government wavered in implementing a minimum wage award decreed by its own appointed commissions.

The focus of such protests is not upon the iniquities of the capitalist system as such but upon the ineptitude, inefficiency, or corruption of the members of the government in power. The vulnerability of the government in such a situation depends variously upon the intensity of the protest and the specificity of the demands; if it can to some extent meet the specific demands protest will be assuaged; if the demands are highly diffuse it will have more opportunity to extricate itself.

The government itself facilitates many of the images outlined in the previous paragraphs; it is in its interest to do so (Ionescu and Gellner, 1969). Its need for popular support has increased in recent decades as universal suffrage has been achieved by the urban poor; the politicians need their votes. The overt support of the poor is needed, too, to maintain credibility within and outside the country. A state racked by industrial unrest will be less likely to attract the foreign investment upon which development plans rest.

Through its control of the mass media the government helps to maintain the dominant ideology. Typical elements are the stress upon achievement, the openness of society and the ability of anyone to reach the top through hard work. The wealth of those at the top is the due reward for their effort. The dependence upon government may be emphasised – benevolence and paternalism blend to suggest that the poor may achieve their goals through co-operation with the government rather than critical attacks on it. Foreign domination provides a convenient scapegoat; but it is the foreignness of the domination, not its capitalist nature, that is emphasised. Failure to support the government over such issues is deemed unpatriotic. Finally, governments themselves accept that their failings are those of inefficiency and corruption. In African states one sees the extreme example as each coup is immediately followed by a purge to cleanse the Augean stables. It is not the system that is at fault – merely the people who run it; they are self-seeking and manipulate the rules for their own personal ends. In contrast, in Latin American states divisions within the dominant strata tend to be more pronounced, and successive governments may be seen to favour one group or policy against another – indigenous businessmen, for example, against foreign investors, state control versus private enterprise.

The leaders of a populist government make more approaches to the poor. Their promises are more widely advertised and will, to a limited extent, be fulfilled. A dialogue may be maintained with representatives of the poor, as the 'government is anxious to understand their problems'. But such dialogues do not give the poor a place in government councils. Ministers seek to identify with the masses – they are photographed wielding a pick or a fork in development projects. In Peru the generals of the military government of 1968-80 frequently appeared in public, not in their full dress uniforms, but in fatigues together with the peasant *poncho*.

The essence of populism, as here defined, is that government leaders, be they elected or military, present themselves as sympathetic to the demands of the poor, avowedly seek to help them and, to some extent, attempt to identify with them. Yet their actions lead to no marked structural change in the society. Wage increases are soon eroded in inflation; glamorous new housing projects provide houses for very few; greater benefits are often won by the middle strata.

One consequence of such a populist policy is that demands by the poor are stimulated, reaching a level that a government, given its other commitments, cannot possibly meet. The government's response is to co-opt, control, or repress. Popular leaders of trade unions, community associations, and the like, are given office within the state bureaucracy and their contact with their erstwhile following is weakened. The masses are thus mobilised 'from above', not 'from below'. Under the aegis of vast community development agencies, such as SINAMOS of Peru (see Dietz, 1980), or single-party machines as in some African states such as Tanzania, local associations are created, often replicating or supplanting autonomous indigenous ones, through which all demands must be articulated; the rewards available are distributed from above. Repression develops as local spokesmen become too vociferous in their demands and are curbed by the supervising officials, through loss of office or, ultimately, imprisonment. In its early years SINAMOS attracted many who saw in it an opportunity to work on behalf of the poor; its ultimate demise came when it was seen in the shanty towns as an agent of police control and an inhibitor of autonomous action.

The violence and brutality of the police and army in Third World states is probably little different from that of their counterparts in nineteenth-century Western Europe; they are, however, very much better equipped and trained to combat urban protest and insurrection.

MOBILISATION FROM ABOVE

Marx anticipated that the workers, through their experience of subordination and exploitation, would develop autonomously a degree of class-consciousness which would enable them to carry out the proletarian revolution. It followed that the revolution would occur first in the more advanced industrial countries. A workers' political party was essential. The role of the party in mobilising the workers then became problematic. Should the party leaders wait for the mass of the workers to develop a high level of class-consciousness before precipitating revolutionary activity? Or should the party constitute the vanguard, perhaps far in advance of its followers?

The debate has become rather sterile as one after another socialist revolution has taken place in a less developed country, and has been led by a small group of intellectuals from the middle strata. These men have usually seen as one of their prime tasks the raising of class-consciousness. As Nkrumah said: 'Seek ye first the political kingdom . . . ' The success of such revolutions has been ascribed by observers not to the class-consciousness of urban workers or peasants, which has admittedly been low, but to the structural coincidence of various contradictions which the ruling groups proved unable to resolve; many of these contradictions concerned the uneven development of the country — the coexistence of traditional and modern structural forms.

The low levels of class-consciousness among the urban poor have already been explained. They are aware of the vast difference in wealth and power between themselves and the dominant groups and may be highly critical of it. Yet the lack of education inhibits their perception of an alternative form of society. Just as peasants are wont to divide the estates which they have seized into individual mini-holdings, resisting government attempts to maintain large-scale and collective farm units, so urban workers aspire to set up their own businesses rather than to organise a co-operative; they seek to return to pre-capitalist modes of production rather than to erect socialist ones. The urban poor are weakly organised; their leadership is often easily co-opted. Poverty, physical tiredness at the end of the day's work, insecurity, all constrain their political activity. Governments hold them in subordination by co-option, repression and ideological dominance.

Yet populist governments have sought the support of the

urban poor. Why have the parties in opposition, and especially those of the radical left, done so little to rally support for their cause? A revolution may be possible before the consciousness of the poor is fully raised. But that does not constitute an argument for failing to attempt to mobilise them. However, in Third World countries very little has been done to mobilise radically the urban poor from above, and radical political parties are conspicuously weak or absent (save, of course, in those countries – Cuba, Mozambique, and so on – where a revolutionary socialist group has seized power).

In Latin American states the rival political parties tend to represent different interest groups within the dominant strata – landowners, indigenous capitalists, professionals dependent on foreign capital. From these interests, together with causes historically associated with the party, stem policies which favour, more or less, the urban poor. In terms of these they are wooed; but these policies do not aim at changing significantly the status of the poor. Only in Chile has a major party sought actively to mobilise the urban masses, but Chile's Indian population is numerically insignificant, and rich and poor both derive from a common European stock. In many other Latin American states economic distinctions are largely congruent with ethnic ones – the rich are white, the poor are Indians or blacks (Handleman, 1975).

In African single-party or military states the party ideology is predominantly nationalistic; a wide spectrum of political positions may be encompassed within it, although perhaps veiled in a radical Marxist rhetoric. Interest cleavages within the dominant groups have not led to the formation of rival political parties; in fact, splits both within and between parties are frequently along ethnic lines, as aspiring leaders try to consolidate their position by winning the overwhelming support of their own ethnic group, with claims that other groups are seeking to dominate them (Markovitz, 1977).

A few political leaders have emerged from the trade union movement – Tom Mboya in Kenya and Sekou Toure in Guinea for examples. But workers' parties have not been formed in Third World states, though some, such as the early APRA in Peru, have relied heavily on trade union support. One obvious reason is the small size of the union-ised working population – too small to ensure victory for a national party. Government co-option and repression have been contributory factors.

Radical political parties tend to be small cliques of middle-strata intellectuals, highly fragmented by divergent political allegiances to Marx, Lenin, Stalin, Trotsky, or Mao. Many develop from student organisations and the turnover of membership is high. Their resources are insuf-ficient for any large-scale activity among the poor. Often they attempt to enhance their standing by exploiting a local and autonomously expressed protest; but their effort to translate the very specific demands of the local protesters into abstract ideological issues, and their supplanting of local leadership on grounds of its inefficiency and lack of experience, tend only to kill the indigenous movement.

Urban guerrilla movements are merely an extreme form of the above; their members would seem to have the same social origins. They seem unable to mobilise the poor, apparently believing that seizure of power can be achieved without such support; and their activities are not approved by the poor.

In Latin America substantial factions within the Roman Catholic Church have ostensibly allied themselves with the poor; Marxism is seen to be compatible with the priesthood. Yet one reads too of the apathy shown by the poor towards the established churches, and of a continuing identification of the church with the dominant groups. Small Protestant sects are developing in the shanty towns, and these tend to support the ideologies of individual achievement. The potential role of the Catholic Church remains problematic: how far can it mobilise the poor, how far can it merely create a more tolerant attitude towards the poor among the higher strata?

The urban poor have been described as opportunistic; they will support those political leaders who promise them rewards, but they quickly reject them if the promises are unfulfilled. They have, in this way, supported at times the most conservative of elected politicians, the most oppressive of military dictators. A reactionary leader who can deliver the goods is to be preferred to the liberal who cannot. But the poor are faced with alternatives which are not of their making; their choices do not reflect their underlying hopes. Thus in recent elections for a Constituent Assembly in Peru radical left-wing leaders won massive support in those suburbs of Lima with a substantial shanty town or worker population. Yet these radicals were unable to unite around a presidential candidate and the victor in the ensuing elections was the very man ousted by the military twelve years previously; the most liberal of the candidates, he had succeeded in part through the support of the urban poor. However, a year later left-wing candidates formed a united front in local government elections and again won massive support among the urban poor. Voting patterns must always be viewed in the context of the choices offered to the electorate.

The activities of the poor, whether these are their struggle to develop their private businesses or their electoral support for conservative politicians, reflect rational ·calculations about the best paths towards the amelioration of their position. Their lack of a perception of an alternative form of society leads them to seek solutions within the present one; and their understanding of this one too is poor. Their lack of organisation inhibits collective activity. But none of these factors negates the intensity of their awareness of their deprivation and subordination in society; they know how poor they are and they wish they were not so. We as observers must try to understand their experience of poverty, their perceptions of its causes and the activities which they deem to be rational responses, in presenting our own explanations.

6

Conclusion

This book has posed an epistemological problem: to what degree can the concepts of class, developed in the past century and a half in the industrial societies of Western Europe, be usefully applied in the urban centres of the Third World nations? More specifically, is there in these cities a working class similar in character to that of our own societies? Or does the employment of our concepts obscure and confuse the realities of development in these cities? Are their urban poor a proletariat? Can their reactions to poverty and inequality be described as class conflict?

Such questions lead to others. Does the pattern of industrialisation in the Third World so parallel that of the West in the nineteenth century that we should expect the development of similar social forms? Secondly, do the Third World urban poor themselves interpret their situation in a manner shared by external observers? For it is an assumption here that a knowledge of the perceptions of actors is essential to an understanding of events.

In some ways the cities of the Third World do resemble those of nineteeth-century Europe. Disraeli's image of the two nations, however, is much more appropriate to the Third World metropolis, with its glaring inequalities between rich and poor, than to contemporary Western societies. In the former a senior professional person commonly earns thirty times the income of an unskilled worker on the national minimal wage. (The corresponding factor in Britain today would be about five.) In these nations it is common for the bottom 60 per cent of the population to receive only 20 per cent of the national income, the top 10 per cent to receive 50 per cent of it. Poverty is not only relative but absolute – the national minimum wage corresponds, in many areas, to £200 or £300 per annum. Our term 'the urban poor' embraces 60 per cent or more of the city population; the poor may well have an average income substantially below the minimum wage. Such poverty is correlated with powerlessness, associated with ignorance through lack of education, with insecurity and long working hours which inhibit political action, and with associational activity directed to competition for benefits among the poor (Miliband, 1974).

But the development of these cities has been consequent and dependent upon the growth of Western industrial society; they have been penetrated by it. In many ways they resemble contemporary Western cities. Their skyscrapers and urban motorways are similar; their upper strata enjoy very similar living styles. Western ideals of universal suffrage and social services are honoured, at least in name. The contrast between modern and traditional is a not entirely inappropriate descriptive device. But as we have seen in earlier chapters the notion that the traditional sector is a relic of the past, likely to wither away in the coming decades, is misleading. It should, in its urban manifestations, be seen as a creation of the modern sector and a necessary and continuing adjunct to it for as long as the present mode of economic development continues. The size of the informal sector as it is described would be paralleled in nineteenth-century Western cities – see, for example, Stedman Jones's (1971) description of *Outcast London*. But the persistence of ethnicity is a new feature, reflecting the need both to retain rights to land in the rural area and to ensure a measure of security in the city. The shanty towns, too, with their heterogeneous income structure and strong associations, are a novel feature. The political structure of Third World states differs in many significant respects: governments have responsibility for many spheres and aspects of the economy – although their degree of control might seem minimal; they are major employers of labour and cannot remain as mere arbiters between industrial employer and employee; they are dependent, too, upon the votes of the poor, both in city and countryside, and so woo their electorates with promises of increased social services – all of which serves to increase their involvement in the economy and in employment. In this they resemble contemporary Western governments – the difference lies in the poverty which constrains their activity.

The economic subordination of the urban poor takes two forms. Some are employed in technologically advanced activities and so have a high productivity; they tend to receive wages which are high relative to the incomes of the urban poor, though low by Western standards. Far more, however, are engaged in technologically primitive forms of activity, and in addition are grossly underemployed; their poverty derives from their low productivity. But it is the economic policies of governments which determine the degree to which such activity shall persist and which constrain, in effect, the efforts of those so employed to improve their conditions.

Our second question concerns the manner in which the urban poor perceive their situation of inequality. Much of the recent literature on actors' images of class has assumed that specific categories of worker each employ different models of the stratification system. This seems, to me, an erroneous approach; we should instead expect people to employ a variety of models, each appropriate to specific contexts. Furthermore, each of these models should reflect not only the work situation but the totality of the experiences of the urban poor. Thus we must take cognisance of their rural origins, their achievement in adjusting to urban life, their associational links in the city, the variety of occupations both within the lifetime of an individual and within his immediate family.

The urban poor are well aware of their poverty and are anxious to rise above it; a number of strategies seem available to them and these involve different ways of looking at the world. In common with individuals everywhere, they can take an ego-centred view of the world, or they can view it as external observers. The two stereotypes, widely reported in the literature and summarised in the previous chapter, are thus not necessarily incompatible with one another, and may certainly coexist. The one stresses the achievement orientation of the poor, their 'petit bourgeois' attitudes; the other the 'proletarian' opposition to government.

In using an ego-centred model the individual sees himself surrounded by his personal network of kin, compatriots, neighbours, patrons and clients. These are, to him, a resource to be used in getting ahead or in merely retaining his social position. Beyond those concentric circles which comprise the 'us' of his world lie 'them' – the upper strata of society, the drop-outs at the lower end and, horizontally, members of similar though unrelated social groupings. Mobility is possible within the 'us' category, difficult or unwelcome beyond it. Within it people are stratified, ladderwise, according to wealth and social prestige. Consumption criteria prevail over those of production.

The same individual may also employ a model in which the 'common people' are seen in opposition to 'government' – a simple dichotomy in which power is at least implicit as a defining criterion. To some extent the relationship between the two entities is one of conflict, but the expression of this conflict may be muted. To the urban poor 'the government' is a rather vague and ill-defined category; they are not sure who does what. Government does not necessarily lack legitimacy. The right to rule may be a just reward for skill and long years of training. Alternative political structures are not understood and so the evils of any government are seen, not in terms of structural contradictions, but in terms of the personal failings of its members, such as their inefficiency or corruption; the solution lies, therefore, in a change of government personnel, not of the economic and social system.

The two models are linked in that the constraints imposed by the overall structure of society promote or inhibit the success which the individual is striving to achieve. We must all have a view of the world as it is, because it is within this world that we operate. We have, too, a view of the world as it might be, perhaps a substantially different world. Our characterisation of the world and of the means of changing it determines our own activities.

TERMINOLOGIES

Let us now turn to our main problem – the appropriateness of terms such as working class and proletariat in designating the urban poor. We must bear in mind the criteria discussed in Chapter 2 in defining classes – in terms of production relationships, of consumption and life-styles, the consciousness of class members of their position in society, and the degree to which class membership is useful in predicting behaviour or in interpreting the course of history.

The pattern of income distribution, with the rich so sharply distinguished from the poor, together with the former's obvious monopoly of power, lends itself to the use of a dichotomous model of society. The terms bourgeoisie and proletariat are quickly offered.

But the dominant group is certainly not a bourgeoisie in the strict Marxist sense of that term; it owns neither the productive wealth of the expatriate companies nor that of the peasants and artisans. The true national bourgeoisie, the indigenous owners of companies independent of, and perhaps opposed to, the expatriate firms, is only a small and frequently insignificant faction in the dominant stratum. For the politicians, civil servants and professionals who do comprise the greater part of this stratum, the term *comprador* bourgeoisie has been used. That debate falls, however, outside the scope of this book.

The term working class has been used to embrace all the poor – whether wage-earners, artisans and petty traders, or peasants – on the ground that all are exploited in various ways. All are indeed poor, but their economic interests and life-styles are so varied that such a blanket term loses more in obscuring differences than it gains in stressing a uniformity. The even more precise connotations of the term proletariat become quite incongruous when applied to peasants!

Let us, however, confine ourselves to the *urban* poor and look first of all at wage employees who might well be designated a working class or proletariat. Remember, however, the range of wage-earning situations: the relatively well-paid workers in stable employment in big companies, the casually employed and unskilled workers in the public services, the employees of small-scale artisans.

In many ways such employees have been held to deviate from our stereotype (Touraine and Pecaut, 1970; McGee, 1973, 1977; Sandbrook, 1975; Waterman, 1975b, 1977, 1978; Elkan, 1976). First, they are not fully committed to urban wage employment. Many still retain land in the rural areas; more hope to retire to their natal town or village. The insecurity of urban life necessitates strong ties with compatriots, which further enhance the bonds with the village. Lack of commitment to wage-earning is further evidenced in the desire to become self-employed in some informal sector activity. The reaction to the subordination implied in wage employment is thus to evade rather than oppose it.

Secondly, in both domestic groups and the local community wage-earning coexists with self-employment. The attitudes and opinions generated in these groups are those appropriate to the informal sector – especially when it is this sector which appears to provide the best avenues for advancement. Some scholars have, indeed, found that radical political attitudes come to predominate only in those residential areas where wage-earners constitute a majority.

Thirdly, as we have seen, those in well-paid, stable employment tend to be well organised in trade unions. But union membership and allegiance is weak among both the unskilled and casually employed and those in small enterprises where paternalistic relationships predominate. Other modes of organisation, such as the ethnic and community associations, serve their members' needs for security and basic services. These are incompatible with trade unions in as much as resources of time, money and energy are scarce. They also promote a different structuring of society – in terms of rival ethnic groups or local communities.

Finally, as has already been described, the focus of

opposition and discontent is 'government', not 'capitalism'. And in the Third World there is less congruence between these terms than in the West. The issues of poverty are directed more towards consumption criteria than to relationships of production.

It has been argued that these deviations from the stereotype are indeed found among the unskilled, but that the skilled worker in the Third World is, in fact, a true proletarian. Certainly he is more likely to be an active trade unionist and more inclined to see capitalism as his enemy. But, for the most part, it is untrue to assert that such people have ruptured their rural links, abjured their aspirations to self-employment, or withdrawn from ethnic and community associations.

Some situations do counter these generalisations. The miners isolated in the high Andes in their company camps have a long history of militancy, although it seems to have had little impact upon their impoverished conditions. In other situations a nationalistic opposition to expatriate companies intensifies the awareness of exploitation, though it may be the foreignness of the companies, rather than their capitalist structure, which is held to account. Again, where poverty coincides with a darker skin, ethnic and racial awareness enhances the feelings of oppression. But in these situations we must distinguish the observer's interpretation of the protest in class terms, albeit recognising that the actors are hampered by their false consciousness, and the actors' own interpretations of their society using models based not upon class but upon other criteria. The latter will determine their actions, and it is highly problematic whether these will have the same ultimate and unintended consequences as class action would have had.

Two issues follow from this discussion of the wage-earning population: the divisions that exist within it, and the categorisation of the self-employed.

The relatively affluent upper end of the wage-earning population has been termed a 'labour aristocracy'. This, however, is very different from its nineteenth-century Western counterpart which consisted of skilled and independent craftsmen drawn into the factory system (Mackenzie, 1973; Gray, 1974). In the Third World it comprises, according to Arrighi (1970), Arrighi and Saul (1973) and Saul (1975), the skilled technicians in large factories and the sub-elite of clerks and teachers (Waterman, 1975). The relationship between these people and the mass of the urban poor is said to be antagonistic, for their privileged position derives from the taxes and high prices for manufactured goods paid by the latter. Quijano (1974) refers to the increasing competition for such jobs; but one must not confuse envy with structural antagonism. The labour aristocrats, it is argued, strive through their militant action to maintain their privileged position and appear to do little for the mass of the poor. They seek to maintain the structure which maintains their position, rather than overthrow it – they are thus politically conservative (Landsberger, 1967).

The first criticism is directed towards the existence of such an aristocracy among factory workers (the white-collar workers are a separate issue). There are some, in certain industries such as oil, who earn high wages and live in rather exclusive residential areas; but very many employees in the big expatriate companies earn no more than the minimum wage. Many such companies are capital-intensive and the workers' wage is only a small proportion of the cost of the product.

Secondly, these groups tend to be among the most militant – in most senses of the word. It is they who are most exploited and they are conscious of this. Bargaining, however, tends to be confined within the company. Selfishness is also seen in their apparent lack of concern for the poor – but what, in effect, could they do? As we have seen, this militancy is not interpreted by the poor antagonistically – it is viewed as leadership (Peace, 1975). The gains of the privileged are quickly passed to the poor through increased prices in the informal sector and through systems of mutual aid. Social ties between these supposed aristocrats and the poor remain strong.

The top echelons of those usually subsumed within the

labour aristocracy should perhaps be viewed as the equivalent of the Western 'new working class' (Mallet, 1963;
Gallie, 1978) of technicians and white-collar functionaries;
but for the majority of Third World factory workers the use
of this term seems inappropriate.

Those outside the wage-earning sector are more difficult
to categorise. We include here the petty self-employed and
all those who work for them – wage-earners, journeymen,
apprentices, family members. In Chapter 3 we saw how
these enterprises were dependent, in a variety of ways, upon
the formal or capitalist sector, but that they were viewed by
their participants as independent. A variety of terms has
been used to characterise this category.

Some use the criterion of poverty to describe this stratum
as a 'lumpenproletariat'. But some of the self-employed are
not poor, as their incomes exceed those of most manual
wage-earners; this faction may perhaps be termed a petite
bourgeoisie. Lumpenproletariat, to Marx and many others,
denotes a rejection of the dominant values of society – it is
composed of criminals, prostitutes, drug addicts. But only
a very small proportion of the urban poor can fairly be
described thus – most are law-abiding citizens striving to
conform. A consequence of this rejection is that the
lumpenproletariat is a weak ally of the organised working
class – it is more likely to be stimulated to mob violence in
support of conservative leaders. However, for Fanon (1967)
it is the locus of revolutionary activity, rather than the
peasantry or the working class (Worsley, 1972). But neither
of these assumptions about political activity among the
urban poor accords with the descriptions recently provided.
The term lumpenproletariat has little to offer.

Others refer to a 'sub-' or 'proto-proletariat'. Here it is
implied that although the category fails to meet all the
requirements of a proletariat, it is on the way to doing so.
Movement is along several dimensions. There is greater
commitment to urban life and employment; ties with the
rural area, with compatriots, diminish. The self-employed
and their co-workers are as dependent, in degree if not in
form, as the factory worker. Here one needs to distinguish

between movement within an individual career and movement of the category in its entirety. There is at present little evidence that the recent migrant is becoming increasingly committed to urban employment. To the extent that factories displace craftsmen, it is unlikely that the latter are absorbed into the former; the new shoe factory hires school leavers, not cobblers. In a few cities massive investment has reduced the size of the informal sector; in most its continuance seems assured. The implication of a disappearing category seems misconceived; it is a permanent one which may nevertheless share some of the characteristics of a proletariat.

Studies of migrants in European cities have used 'underclass' to describe the foreign workers (Castles and Kosack, 1973). They tend to be at the lowest levels of the work hierarchy; they may be denied certain rights of citizenship; they are rejected by the trade union movement of the dominant race or ethnic group; and in response they turn inwards for support. In many ways one can analyse these groups as one does the ethnic components of the Third World city. But in the latter all the urban poor are 'ethnics'; so under class is not appropriate here.

Latin American scholars have developed the concept of 'marginality' – a common euphemism for the urban poor is *los marginados* (marginals and marginated) (Nun, 1969; Weffort and Quijano, 1973; Germani, 1980). Deriving perhaps from the American concept of the marginal man – sited ambiguously between classes – the term was first used to designate cultural marginality; the migrant adjusting from the traditional norms of his rural home to the Westernised life of the city was seen as marginal. But others have described the urban poor as integrated into city life, sharing its values (Perlman, 1976). Radicals subsequently used the term to demonstrate how the capitalist process excluded the poor from social benefits. But though the term usually seems to refer to the very poor, by definition, it would seem to embrace wage-earners. Alternatively, it may denote those with no economic function in the capitalist system. The 'reserve army of labour' refers to those who gain employment in boom periods and lose it in recessions, but it is a small category. The mass of the urban poor in the self-employed sector are surplus to the requirements of the reserve army; they are thus marginal.

Quijano (1972) has differentiated between the proletariat proper and a marginal proletariat – those insecurely employed and on below-minimum wages; and between the relatively prosperous petite bourgeoisie and the marginal petite bourgeoisie of poor artisans, petty traders, and the like. However, the distinction between marginal and non-marginal seems to be based simply on income and consequent life-style and not on the relationships within the capitalist structures. He does note, however, the substantial social homogeneity of the marginal categories, the movement of persons between occupations, the cross-cutting social ties, the shared view of the world.

In all these attempts to label the self-employed of the informal sector one feels that they are being designated a residual category – a rag-bag which defies classification. If one holds that classes exist only in capitalist society and that the traditional/informal sector is non-capitalist, then this procedure is legitimate. But if one views this sector as being within the overall capitalist structure and if one believes that classes must embrace all members of society, then a classification which fails to cope with such a substantial proportion of the population is in need of revision.

On the other hand, all societies are too complex for any simple categorisation into two or three classes to be entirely satisfying. All societies have, perhaps, a 'fragmentary class structure' (K. Roberts *et al.*, 1977). In Western societies it is the 'middle class' – those who rank below the upper professionals and above those who cannot cope and so rely on social security – which is so difficult to describe; in the Third World it is the equally amorphous mass of the urban poor. Poulantzas's conception of factions and strata may prove useful here, but our description of the urban poor has shown that our subdivisions of this category do not fit neatly into a pyramidal structure. They cross-cut each other in a most complex manner. Our problem here is as Giddens has noted, to equate economic and social categories. To achieve congruence we must perhaps redefine our categories. Our understanding of the world proceeds as we attempt to reduce the number of concepts we use, to simplify the patterns of relationships. But in doing so the departure from reality becomes more obvious, as so many items no longer fit into our neat schema. A new classification must be devised to take account of these.

The foregoing paragraphs will have given the impression that class analysis consists merely of the labelling of social groups and categories. But as Marxists and others argue, class is a force in history; labelling exercises are puerile and sterile (Mamdani, 1975; Shivji, 1976). Indeed, my own position has been that classes exist only in action.

As we have seen, the urban poor of the Third World cities do protest against their subordination, however muted, misdirected, or repressed these attempts may be. There *is* a continual struggle against poverty, both to rise out of it through individual effort and to achieve a more just society.

Some writers would see any such protest as 'class action'; not only is a strike a 'class action' but so is the individual worker's shaking of the fist, or verbal abuse against his employer. On the basis of such actions class-consciousness is said to exist. But Western observers who define class in this manner either stop with the imposition of a label or proceed to assume that the classes have the attributes of those similarly labelled in Western society. Herein lies the danger of departing from reality.

Of what are the actors in the situation conscious – in terms of the models they use, of the processes of subordination which they perceive, of their identification of their enemy? In endorsing the social system which they perceive as legitimate or in expressing subordination in terms of other groupings, of ethnicity, for instance, the external observer may accuse them of false consciousness. But their actions can only be fully understood and explained on the basis both of the actor's consciousness and of the forces of society of which he is not conscious. Our task is not only to assess the degree and mode of subordination and exploitation but also to see how the urban poor themselves conceptualise it, to evaluate the mode of social protest. How far are we entitled to speak of social classes among the urban poor if they do not use our own mode of analysis?

Finally, there are those for whom the revolution itself proves the prior existence of classes. Thus, although most descriptions of Castro's victory in Cuba point to the negligible role of the urban workers, some (Petras, 1978, for example) insist that the events demonstrate the militancy of the proletariat. The concept of 'overdetermination' is useful here. Revolutions have occurred in the Third World because of the multiplicity of factors and situations, broadly associated with the increased incorporation into the capitalist world, with which the dominant groups have been unable to cope in their attempts to maintain their power. But these factors and situations do not have to be expressed in class terms – unless, of course, one is again using class to refer to any form of protest against social inequality.

As we noted earlier, class analysis is itself praxis, an ideology. The discovery of classes is a prescription for action, a basis for prophecy. Assertions of their absence is taken to signify an opposing political stance. But any social movement must surely accommodate both the prophets, with their visions of the apocalyptic future, and the pragmatists, who deliberate the exact character of the route being followed.

In writing this book I have been aware, at many points, that the themes discussed would be equally relevant to studies of our own Western societies – but they have often been neglected in the literature and space prohibits their elaboration here. The focal issues in Third World studies may be the blind spots in Western ones. In part this is due to the salience of certain forms of organisation in the former; to the different intellectual paradigms in the two areas of study; to the larger tradition of ethnographic research (by all social scientists) in the former. Our analysis of social protest in nineteenth-century Europe rests upon documentary evidence, in the contemporary Third World upon participant observation, and the kind of data generated affects the mode of analysis. Third World studies are rich in their descriptions of ethnic and community relationships – the totality of social life and not merely the work situation.

One Western issue which Third World studies might help to clarify is the status of the 'traditional worker'. The cloth-capped militant proletarian is a popular stereotype; Goldthorpe and Lockwood bestowed academic legitimacy on it, Giddens and many others accept the existence of such a figure in the nineteenth century. But Westergaard has argued in theoretical terms that the universalistic class-consciousness imputed could hardly have existed in the last century – it is more a phenomenon of this one. Empirical studies, such as that by Moore (1974) of Durham miners, have failed to find the traditional worker. The stereotype continues, however, especially in postulating the decline of worker militancy through the present century.

Many current aspects of life in Third World cities were perhaps paralleled in those of nineteenth-century Europe; the contemporary descriptions of Dickens and the recent historical analyses of Stedman Jones seem particularly appropriate. In both situations social protest has taken a variety of very similar forms.

The 'decline of militancy' theme in the West is in fact paralleled by the attempts to account for a less than expected militancy among the Third World urban poor. In the 1960s their cities were assumed to be on the verge of an explosion – it was felt that the intolerable poverty experienced would surely lead to violence. The violence rarely materialised; and in attempting to explain this the urban poor have been shown either as passive or as individually achievement-oriented.

In each of these situations we can see an attempt to interpret the absence of violent protest as indicating a complete acquiescence in the structure of society – a universal consensus, or one-class society. But inequality does exist; the underprivileged do protest. We must examine this protest without being blinkered by terminologies of narrow application.

Bibliography

Altamirano, T. (1980), 'Regional commitments and political involvement among migrants in Lima: the case of regional associations', PhD thesis, University of Durham.

Arrighi, G. (1970), 'International corporations, labour aristocracies and economic development in tropical Africa', *Journal of Modern African Studies*, vol. 6, pp. 141–69.

Arrighi, G., and Saul, J. (1973), *Essays in the Political Economy of Africa* (New York: Monthly Review Press).

Bairoch, P. (1973), *Urban Unemployment in Developing Countries* (Geneva: ILO).

Balan, J., Browning, H., and Jelin, E. (1973), *Man in a Developing Society* (Austin, Texas: University of Texas Press).

Basch, L.G. (1978), 'Working for the Yankee dollar: the impact of a transnational petroleum company on Caribbean class and ethnic relations', PhD thesis, New York University.

Benson, L. (1978), *Proletarians and Parties* (London: Tavistock).

Booth, J. A., and Seligson, M. A. (1978), *Political Participation in Latin America, Vol. 1: Citizen and State* (New York: Holmes & Meier).

Bose, A. N. (1974), *The Informal Sector in the Calcutta Metropolitan Economy* (Geneva: ILO).

Bromley, R., and Gerry, C. (eds) (1979), *Casual Work and Poverty in Third World Cities* (Chichester and New York: Wiley).

Bulmer, M. (ed.) (1975), *Working Class Images of Society* (London: Routledge & Kegan Paul).

Cardoso, F. H., and Faletto, E. (1969), *Dependencia y Desarrollo en Americana Latina* (Mexico City: Siglo Veintiuno).

Castells, M. (1977), *The Urban Question: A Marxist Approach* (London: Edward Arnold).

Castles, S., and Kosack, G. (1973), *Immigrant Workers and Class Structures in Western Europe* (London: OUP).

Clark, S. (1978), 'The importance of agrarian classes: agrarian class structure and collective action in nineteenth-century Ireland', *British Journal of Sociology*, vol. 29, no. 1, pp. 22–40.

Cohen, A. (ed.) (1974), *Urban Ethnicity* (London: Tavistock).

Cohen, R. (1972), 'Class in Africa: analytical problems and perspectives', in R. Miliband and J. Saville (eds), *The Socialist Register 1972* (London: Merlin Press).

Cohen, R. (1974), *Labour and Politics in Nigeria* (London: Heinemann).

Cohen, R., Weeks, J. F., and Kilby, P. (1971), 'Further comment on the Kilby/Weeks debate', *Journal of Developing Areas*, vol. 5, pp. 155–76.

Cornelius, W. A. (1970), 'Political sociology of cityward migration in Latin America: toward empirical theory' in F. R. Rabinowitz and F. M. Trueblood (eds), *Latin American Urban Research 1* (Beverly Hills, Calif.: Sage).

Cornelius, W. A. (1975), *Politics and the Migrant Poor in Mexico City* (Stanford, Calif.: Stanford University Press).

Cowley, J., Kaye, A., Mayo, M., and Thompson, M. (1977), *Community or Class Struggle* (London: Stage 1).

Crompton, R., and Gubbay, J. (1977), *Economy and Class Structure* (London: Macmillan).

Dahrendorf, R. (1959), *Class and Class Conflict in Industrial Society* (Stanford, Calif.: Stanford University Press).

Davies, I. (1966), *African Trade Unions* (Harmondsworth: Penguin).

Davis, H. H. (1979), *Beyond Class Images* (London: Croom Helm).

Dietz, H. A. (1980), *Poverty and Problem-Solving under Military Rule: The Urban Poor in Lima, Peru* (Austin, Texas: University of Texas Press).

Diop, A. (1960), 'Enquête sur la migration Toucouleur à Dakar', *Bulletin de l'IFAN,* vol. 22, ser. B.

Eames, E., and Goode, J. G. (1973), *Urban Poverty in a Cross Cultural Context* (New York: The Free Press).

Eckstein, S. (1977), *The Poverty of Revolution: The State and the Urban Poor in Mexico* (Princeton, NJ: Princeton University Press).

Elkan, W. (1976), 'Is a proletariat emerging in Nairobi?', *Economic Development and Cultural Change*, vol. 24, pp. 695–706.

Epstein, A. L. (1958), *Politics in an Urban African Community* (Manchester: Manchester University Press).

Fanon, F. (1967), *The Wretched of the Earth* (Harmondsworth: Penguin).

Foster-Carter, A. (1978), 'The modes of production controversy', *New Left Review*, vol. 107, pp. 47–77.

Frank, A. G. (1969), *Capitalism and Underdevelopment in Latin America* (New York: Monthly Review Press).

Frank, A. G. (1972), *Lumpen Bourgeoisie – Lumpen Development* (New York: Monthly Review Press).

Friedland, W. (1969), *Vuta Kamba: The Development of Trade Unions in Tanganyika* (Stanford, Calif.: Stanford University Press).

Gallie, D. (1978), *In Search of the New Working Class* (Cambridge: CUP).

Geertz, C. (1963), *Pedlars and Princes: Social Development and Economic Change in Two Indonesian Towns* (Chicago: University of Chicago Press).

Germani, G. (1980), *Marginality* (New Brunswick, NJ: Transaction Books).

Gerry, C. (1974), *Petty Producers and the Urban Economy: A Case Study of Dakar* (Geneva: ILO, World Employment Survey).

Giddens, A. (1973), *The Class Structure of the Advanced Societies* (London: Hutchinson).

Gilbert, A. (1974), *Latin American Development: A Geographical Perspective* (Harmondsworth: Penguin).

Goldthorpe, J., Lockwood, D., Bechhofer, F., and Platt, J. (1969), *The Affluent Worker in the Class Structure* (Cambridge: CUP).

Goldthorpe, J. H. (1980), *Social Mobility and Class Structure in Modern Britain* (Oxford: Clarendon Press).

Gray, R. (1974), 'The labour aristocracy in the Victorian class structure', in F. Parkin (ed.), *The Social Analysis of Class Structure* (London: Tavistock).

Grillo, R. D. (1973), *African Railwaymen: Solidarity and Opposition in an East African Labour Force* (Cambridge: CUP).

Grillo, R. D. (1974), *Race Class and Militancy: An African Trade Union 1939–1965* (New York: Chandler).

Gupta, D. (1978), 'The causes and constraints of an Indian social movement', in S. Saberwal (ed.), *Process and Institution in Urban India* (New Delhi: Vikas).

Gutkind, P. C. W. (1973), 'From the energy of despair to the anger of despair: the transition from social circulation to political consciousness among the urban poor in Africa', *Canadian Journal of African Studies*, vol. 7, pp. 179–98.

Gutkind, P. C. W. (1975), 'The view from below: political consciousness of the urban poor in Ibadan', *Cahiers d'études africaines,* vol. 16, pp. 5–35.

Gutkind, P. C. W., and Waterman, P. (1977), *African Social Studies: A Radical Reader* (London: Heinemann).

Gutkind, P. C. W., Cohen, R., and Copans, J. (eds) (1978), *African Labour History* (Beverly Hills, Calif.: Sage).

Handleman, H. (1975), 'The political mobilization of urban squatter settlements', *Latin American Research Review*, vol. 10, pp. 35–72.

Hart, K. (1973), 'Informal income opportunities and urban employment in Ghana', *Journal of Modern African Studies*, vol. 11, pp. 61–89.

Hindess, B., and Hirst, P. Q. (1975), *Pre-Capitalist Modes of Production* (London: Routledge & Kegan Paul).

Holmström, M. (1976), *South Indian Factory Workers: Their Life and their World* (Cambridge: CUP).

Horowitz, I. L. (ed.) (1970), *Masses in Latin America* (New York: OUP).

Hunt, A. (ed.) (1977), *Class and Class Structure* (London: Lawrence & Wishart).

International Labour Organisation (1972), *Employment, Incomes and Equality: A Strategy for Increasing Productive Employment in Kenya* (Geneva: ILO).

Ionescu, G., and Gellner, E. (eds) (1969), *Populism: Its Meanings and National Characteristics* (London: Weidenfeld & Nicolson).

Jeffries, R. (1978), *Class, Power and Ideology in Ghana: The Railwaymen of Sekondi* (Cambridge: CUP).

Jongkind, F. (1974), 'A reappraisal of the role of regional associations in

Lima, Peru: an epistemological perspective', *Comparative Studies in Society and History*, vol. 16, no. 4.

King, K. J. (1977), *The African Artisan: Education and the Informal Sector in Kenya* (London: Heinemann).

Kitching, G. (1972), 'Concept of class and the study of Africa', *The African Review*, no. 3, pp. 327–50.

Kitching, G. (1977), 'Modes of production and Kenyan dependency', *Review of African Political Economy*, vol. 8, pp. 56–74.

Kitching, G. (1980), *Class and Economic Change in Kenya: The Making of an African Petite-Bourgeoisie* (New Haven, Conn.: Yale University Press).

Laclau, E. (1971), 'Federalism and capitalism in Latin America', *New Left Review*, no. 67, pp. 19–38.

Laite, J. (1981), *Industrial Development and Migrant Labour* (Manchester: Manchester University Press).

Landsberger, H. A. (1967), 'The labour elite: is it revolutionary?', in S. M. Lipset and A. Solari (eds), *Elites in Latin America* (New York: OUP).

Leacock, E. (ed.) (1971), *The Culture of Poverty: A Critique* (New York: Simon & Schuster).

Le Brun, O., and Gerry, C. (1975), 'Petty producers and capitalism', *Review of African Political Economy*, vol. 3, pp. 20–32.

Lewis, O. (1967), *La Vida: A Puerto Rican Family in the Culture of Poverty* (London: Secker & Warburg).

Leys, C. (1973), 'Interpreting African underdevelopment: reflections on the ILO report on employment, incomes and equality in Kenya', *African Affairs*, vol. 72, pp. 419–29.

Lipset, S. M., and Solari, A. (eds) (1967), *Elites in Latin America* (New York: OUP).

Lloyd, P. C. (ed.) (1966), *The New Elites of Tropical Africa* (London: OUP).

Lloyd, P. C. (1967), *Africa in Social Change* (Harmondsworth: Penguin).

Lloyd, P. C. (1974), *Power and Independence: Urban Africans' Perceptions of Social Inequality* (London: Routledge & Kegan Paul).

Lloyd, P. C. (1979), *Slums of Hope?: Shanty Towns of the Third World* (Harmondsworth: Penguin).

Lloyd, P. C. (1980), *The 'Young Towns' of Lima: Aspects of Urbanization in Peru* (Cambridge: CUP).

Lomnitz, L. (1977), *Networks and Marginality: Life in a Mexican Shanty Town* (New York: Academic Press).

Lubeck, P. (1978), 'Labour in Kano since the petroleum boom', *Review of African Political Economy*, vol. 13, pp. 37–46.

Lubeck, P. (1979), 'Class formation and the periphery: class consciousness and Islamic nationalism among Nigerian workers', in R. L. and I. H. Simpson (eds), *Research in the Sociology of Work: Worker Consciousness* (Greenwich, Conn.: JAI Press).

Lynch, O. M. (1969), *The Politics of Untouchability* (New York: Columbia University Press).

Lynch, O. M. (1974), 'Political mobilisation and ethnicity among Adi-Dravidas in a Bombay slum', *Economic and Political Weekly*, vol. 9, no. 39.

Lynch, O. M. (1979), 'Potters, plotters, prodders in a Bombay slum', *Urban Anthropology*, vol. 8, no. 1, pp. 1–27.

MacEwen, A. (1974), 'Differentiation among the urban poor in an Argentine shanty town', in E. de Kadt and G. Williams (eds), *Sociology and Development* (London: Tavistock).

McGee, T. G. (1973), 'Peasants in cities: a paradox, a most ingenious paradox', *Human Organisation*, vol. 32, pp. 135–42.

McGee, T. G. (1977), 'The persistence of the proto-proletariat: occupational structures and planning of the future of Third World cities', in J. Abu-Lughod and R. Hay (eds), *Third World Urbanization* (Chicago: Maaroufa Press).

Mackenzie, G. (1973), *The Aristocracy of Labour* (Cambridge: CUP).

Mallet, S. (1963), *La Nouvelle Classe ouvrière* (Paris: Editions de Seuil).

Mamdani, M. (1975), 'Class struggles in Uganda', *Review of African Political Economy*, vol. 4, pp. 26–61.

Mangin, W. (1967), 'Latin American squatter settlement: a problem and a solution', *Latin American Research Review*, vol. 2, no. 3.

Mangin, W. (ed.) (1970), *Peasants in Cities* (Boston, Mass.: Houghton Mifflin).

Mann, M. (1973), *Consciousness and Action among the Western Working Class* (London: Macmillan).

Markovitz, I. L. (1977), *Power and Class in Africa* (Englewood Cliffs, NJ: Prentice-Hall).

Mayer, P. (1961), *Townsmen or Tribesmen* (Capetown: OUP).

Miliband, R. (1969), *The State in Capitalist Society* (London: Weidenfeld & Nicolson).

Miliband, R. (1971), 'Barnave: a case of bourgeois class consciousness', in I. Meszaros (ed.), *Aspects of History and Class Consciousness* (London: Routledge & Kegan Paul).

Miliband, R. (1974), 'Politics and poverty', in D. Wedderburn (ed.), *Poverty, Inequality and Class Structure* (Cambridge: CUP), pp. 183–96.

Mitchell, J. C. (1969), *Social Networks in Urban Situations: Analysis of Personal Relationships in Central African Towns* (Manchester: Manchester University Press).

Moore, R. S. (1974), *Pitmen, Preachers and Politics: The Effects of Methodism in a Durham Mining Community* (Cambridge: CUP).

Moorhouse, H. F. (1976), 'Attitudes to class and class relationships in Britain', *Sociology*, vol. 10, no. 3, pp. 469–96.

Moser, C. (1976), *The Informal Sector or Petty Commodity Production: Autonomy or Dependence in Urban Development* (London: University College, Development Planning Unit).

Moser, C. (1977), 'The dual economy and marginality debate and the contribution of micro-analysis: market sellers in Bogota', *Development and Change*, vol. 8, no. 4, pp. 465–89.

Nair, K. S. (1978), *Ethnicity and Urbanization: A Case Study of the Ethnic Identity of South Indian Migrants in Poona* (Delhi: Ajanta).

Nash, J. (1979), *We Eat the Mines and the Mines Eat Us: Dependency and Exploitation in Bolivian Tin Mines* (New York: Columbia University Press).

Nelson, J. M. (1979), *Access to Power: Politics and the Urban Poor in Developing Nations* (Princeton, NJ: Princeton University Press).

Nun, J. (1969), 'Sobre población relativa, ejército industrial de reserva y masa marginal', *Revista Latinoamericana de sociologia*, vol. 4, no. 2, pp. 178–237.

O'Brien, P. J. (1975), 'A critique of Latin American theories of dependency', in I. Oxaal, T. Barett and D. Booth (eds), *Beyond the Sociology of Development* (London: Routledge & Kegan Paul).

Ossowski, S. (1963), *Class Structure in the Social Consciousness* (London: Routledge & Kegan Paul).

Parkin, F. (1971), *Class Inequality and Political Order* (London: MacGibbon & Kee).

Parkin, F. (1974a), 'Strategies of social closure in class formation', in F. Parkin (ed.), *The Social Analysis of Class Structure* (London: Tavistock).

Parkin, F. (1974b) (ed.), *The Social Analysis of Class Structure* (London: Tavistock).

Payne, J. L. (1965), *Labour and Politics in Peru: The System of Political Bargaining* (New Haven, Conn.: Yale University Press).

Peace, A. J. (1974), 'Industrial protest in Nigeria', in E. de Kadt and G. Williams (eds), *Sociology and Development* (London: Tavistock).

Peace, A. J. (1975), 'The Lagos proletariat: labour aristocrats or populist militants?', in R. Sandbrook and R. Cohen (eds), *The Development of an African Working Class* (London: Longman).

Peace, A. J. (1979), *Choice, Class and Conflict: A Study of Southern Nigerian Factory Workers* (Brighton: Harvester).

Peattie, L. R. (1968), *The View from the 'Barrio'* (Ann Arbor, Mich.: University of Michigan Press).

Peil, M. (1972), *The Ghanaian Factory Worker* (Cambridge: CUP).

Perlman, J. (1976), *The Myth of Marginality* (Berkeley, Calif.: University of California Press).

Petras, J. (1978), 'Socialist revolutions and their class components', *New Left Review*, no. 111, pp. 37–66.

Pickvance, C. G. (ed.) (1976), *Urban Sociology: Critical Essays* (London: Tavistock).

Portes, A. (1972), 'Rationality in the slum: an essay on interpretive sociology', *Comparative Studies in Society and History*, vol. 14, no. 3, pp. 268–86.

Poulantzas, N. (1973a), *Political Power and Social Classes* (London: New Left Books).

Poulantzas, N. (1973b), 'On Social Classes', *New Left Review*, no. 78, pp. 27–54.

Quijano, A. (1972), 'La constitucion del "mundo" de la marginalidad urbana', *Revista Latinoamericana de estudias urbano regionales*, vol. 2, pp. 89–106.

Quijano, A. (1974), 'The marginal pole of the economy and the marginalised labour force', *Economy and Society*, vol. 3, no. 4, pp. 393–428.

Remy, D. (1975), 'Economic security and industrial unionism: a Nigerian case study', in R. Sandbrook and R. Cohen (eds), *The Development of an African Working Class* (London: Longman).

Rex, J. (1961), *Key Problems in Sociological Theory* (London: Routledge & Kegan Paul).

Richardson, C. J. (1977), *Contemporary Social Mobility* (London: Frances Pinter).

Roberts, B. (1973), *Organising Strangers* (Austin, Texas: University of Texas Press).

Roberts, B. (1974), 'The interrelationships of city and provinces in Peru and Guatemala', in W. Cornelius and F. Trueblood (eds), *Latin American Urban Research*, Vol. 4 (Beverly Hills, Calif.: Sage), pp. 207–36.

Roberts, B. (1978), *Cities of Peasants* (London: Edward Arnold).

Roberts, K., Cook, F. G., Clarke, S. C., and Semeonoff, E. (1977), *The Fragmentary Class Structure* (London: Heinemann).

Ross, M. H. (1973), *The Political Integration of Urban Squatters* (Evanston, Ill.: Northwestern University Press).

Roxborough, I. (1979), *Theories of Underdevelopment* (London: Macmillan).

Runciman, W. G. (1966), *Relative Deprivation and Social Justice* (London: Routledge & Kegan Paul).

Sandbrook, R. (1975), *Proletarians and African Capitalism: The Kenyan Case* (Cambridge: CUP).

Sandbrook, R., and Arn, J. (1977), *The Labouring Poor and Urban Class Formation: The Case of Greater Accra*, Occasional Monograph Series, No. 2 (Montreal: McGill University, Centre for Developing Areas Studies).

Sandbrook, R., and Cohen, R. (eds) (1975), *The Development of an African Working Class* (London: Longman).

Santos, M. (1979), *The Shared Space: The Two Currents of the Urban Economy in Underdeveloped Countries* (London: Methuen).

Saul, J. S. (1975), 'The "labour aristocracy" thesis reconsidered', in R. Sandbrook and R. Cohen (eds), *The Development of an African Working Class* (London: Longman), pp. 303–10.

Seligson, M. A., and Booth, J. A. (1979), *Political Participation in Latin America, Volume II: Politics and the Poor* (New York: Holmes & Meier).

Sengupta, A. K. (1978), 'Trade unions, politics and the state: a case from West Bengal', in S. Saberwal (ed.), *Process and Institution in Urban India* (New Delhi: Vikas).

Sheth, N. R. (1968), *The Social Framework of an Indian Factory* (Bombay: OUP).

Shivji, I. (1976), *Class Struggles in Tanzania* (London: Heinemann).

Singh, A. M. (1976), *Neighbourhood and Social Networks in Urban India* (New Delhi: Marwah Publications).

Skeldon, R. (1976), 'Regional associations and population migration in Peru: an interpretation', *Urban Anthropology*, vol. 5, no. 3.

Skeldon, R. (1977), 'Regional associations: a note on opposed interpretation', *Comparative Studies in Society and History*, vol. 19, no. 4, pp. 506–10.

Smith, G. A. (1975), 'The social basis of peasant political activity: the case of the Huasicanchinos of central Peru', D Phil thesis, University of Sussex.

Southall, A. (ed.), (1973), *Urban Anthropology: Cross Cultural Studies of Urbanization* (New York: OUP).

Stedman Jones, G. (1971), *Outcast London* (Oxford: Clarendon Press).

Strickon, A. (1967), 'Folk models of stratification', in P. Halmos (ed.), *Latin American Sociological Studies,* Sociological Review Monograph, No. 11 (Keele: University of Keele).

Sulmont, D. (1975), *El movimiento obrero en el Peru 1900–1906* (Lima: Pontificia Universidad Catolica del Peru).

Swainson, N. (1977), 'The rise of a national bourgeoisie in Kenya', *Review of African Political Economy*, vol. 8, pp. 39–55.

Terray, E. (1975), 'Classes and class consciousness in the Abron kingdom of Gyaman', in M. Bloch (ed.), *Marxist Analyses and Social Anthropology* (London: Malaby Press).

Touraine, A. (1976), *Les Sociétés dépendantes* (Paris: Duculot).

Touraine, A., and Pecaut, D. (1970), 'Working class consciousness and economic development in Latin America', in I.L. Horowitz (ed.), *Masses in Latin America* (New York: OUP).

Warner, W. L. (1949), *Social Class in America* (Chicago: Science Research Associates, Inc.).

Waterman, P. (1975a), 'The "labour aristocracy" in Africa: introduction to a debate', *Development and Change*, vol. 6, no. 3, pp. 57–73.

Waterman, P. (1975b), *Third World Workers: An Overview*, Working Paper No. 9 (Montreal: McGill University, Centre for Developing Areas).

Waterman, P. (1977), 'Workers in the Third World', *Monthly Review*, vol. 29, no. 4, pp. 50–64.

Waterman, P. (1978), 'Consciousness, organisation and action amongst Lagos port workers', *Review of African Political Economy*, vol. 13, pp. 47–62.

Weffort, F. C. and Quijano, A. (eds) (1973), *Populismo, marginali-*

zacion y dependencia (San José, Costa Rica: Editorial Universitaria Centroamericana).

Wells, F. A., and Warmington, W. A. (1962), *Studies in Industrialization: Nigeria and the Cameroons* (London: OUP).

Wesolowski, W. (1979), *Classes, Strata and Power* (London: Routledge & Kegan Paul).

Westergaard, J., and Resler, H. (1975), *Class in a Capitalist Society: A Study of Contemporary Britain* (London: Heinemann).

Wiebe, P. D. (1975), *Social Life in an Indian Slum* (New Delhi: Vikas).

Williams, G. (1974), 'Political consciousness among the Ibadan poor', in E. de Kadt and G. Williams (eds), *Sociology and Development* (London: Tavistock).

Wolpe, H. (1970), 'Some problems concerning revolutionary consciousness', in R. Miliband and J. Savile (eds), *The Socialist Register* (London: Merlin Press).

Worsley, P. (1972), 'Franz Fanon and the lumpen proletariat', in R. Miliband and J. Savile (eds), *The Socialist Register 1972* (London: Merlin Press).

Zeitlin, M. (1967), *Revolutionary Politics and the Cuban Working Class* (Princeton, NJ: Princeton University Press).

Zenteno, R.B. (ed.) (1973) *Las clases sociales en America Latina* (Mexico: Siglo Veintiuno).

Zenteno, R. B. (ed.) (1977), *Clases sociales y crisis politica en America Latina* (Mexico: Siglo Veintiuno).

Index